LOVING
FOR
REAL

Father Pierre-Hervé Grosjean

A Crossroad Book
The Crossroad Publishing Company
New York

The Crossroad Publishing Company
www.CrossroadPublishing.com
© 2018 by Pierre-Hervé Grosjean
Crossroad, Herder & Herder, and the crossed C logo/colophon are
registered trademarks of The Crossroad Publishing Company.

All rights reserved. No part of this book may be copied, scanned,
reproduced in any way, or stored in a retrieval system, or transmit-
ted, in any form or by any means, electronic, mechanical, photo-
copying, recording, or otherwise, without the written permission of
The Crossroad Publishing Company. For permission, please write to
rights@crossroadpublishing.com.

In continuation of our 200-year tradition of independent publishing,
The Crossroad Publishing Company proudly offers a variety of books
with strong, original voices and diverse perspectives. The viewpoints
expressed in our books are not necessarily those of The Crossroad
Publishing Company, any of its imprints or of its employees, execu-
tives, owners. Although the author and publisher have made every
effort to ensure that the information in this book was correct at press
time, the author and publisher do not assume and hereby disclaim
any liability to any party for any loss, damage, or disruption caused by
errors or omissions, whether such errors or omissions result from neg-
ligence, accident, or any other cause. No claims are made or responsibility assumed for any health or other benefits.

All rights reserved for all countries
© April 2014, Editions Artège, France
Editions Artège
9, Espace Méditerranée – 66000 Perpignan
www.editionsartege.fr

Book design by Tim Holtz Design
Cover Design: George Forster

Library of Congress Cataloging-in-Publication Data available from
the Library of Congress.

ISBN 978-0-8245-2360-2

Books published by The Crossroad Publishing Company may be pur-
chased at special quantity discount rates for classes and institutional
use. For information, please email sales@CrossroadPublishing.com.

Dedication

For my parents, who taught me
what it means to "love."
For Father Francis, a priest with
the heart of an educator
and a Father.
For Pierre, Guillaume, Yves,
Marc, Pierre, Gérald
priestly brothers who watch over
me and encourage me!
For my parishioners, and for my bishop
who entrusted them to me.
For these girls and boys
who I was able to receive, to
listen to, and to accompany.
For these young people who, in
spite of their weaknesses,
marked me with their generosity,
their great desire for love
and thirst for the absolute.
For all those who have given me
the joy of offering them
God's forgiveness.
For them, I am happy to be a priest.
Thank you.

Contents

Preface

On June 1, 1980, the soon-to-be-canonized John Paul II stopped in at the *Parc des Princes* one memorable Sunday evening while on a visit to France. There he addressed the young people of France, as he would do so often during World Youth Day.

The youth listened and applauded while he recalled the commandments and guidance of the Gospel.

"Your problems and your young sufferings are known to me. . . . You already know all this to the point of being saturated. I prefer to reach for the stars with you. I am convinced that you are seeking to get away from this debilitating atmosphere and that you want to deepen or rediscover the sense of a truly human existence because it is open to God—in a word, you want to rediscover your human vocation in Christ. . . . Jesus did not come to condemn love but to release love from its ambiguities and its counterfeits."[1]

Because we all need to be clearly informed about things while remaining connected to our deep desire for love.

Father Pierre-Hervé Grosjean, priest of the "John Paul II generation," meets regularly with young people. He listens and talks to them—directly and respectfully—by tapping into the richness of wisdom.

As I read Father Grosjean, I recall once again the words of John Paul II to the young people, inviting them not to forget neither their intelligence, nor their hearts, nor their bodies. . . . "Adoration of the body? No, never! Contempt of the body? Even less. Mastery of the body! Yes! Transfiguration of the body! Even more!"[2]

Eric Aumonier,
Bishop of Versailles

Introduction

Why This Book?

Ten years ago, at the invitation of *Les jeunes témoins de la vie humaine*[1] who were organizing their national weekend and a few months before my priestly ordination, I gave a kind of improvised talk on "flirting." The word itself is now somewhat outdated. A year later, a young man asked me if he could give a copy of the talk to one of his friends. The Internet's magic did not take long to have an effect; the talk was widely circulated, which resulted in me receiving numerous letters and invitations to speak at high schools. Some years later, I gave a lecture to students at the Saint-Augustin Parish in Paris entitled "Loving for Real." The experience of several years of priesthood then allowed me to adjust certain things and go a little more deeply into the topic. Again, the audio recording and the text of this talk have circulated extensively.[2] I have since had the opportunity to regularly intervene in parishes or schools. I receive emails almost daily from young people who received a copy of the talk through a friend and who let me know what they have learned. I have been witness to an amazing fertility that is completely beyond me and that points to the Internet as an additionally formidable tool for the apostolate, including the spreading of information among friends.

From these letters and these talks I have distilled a couple of important lessons. First, there is the heaviness of some misconceptions. They significantly blur the understanding of the Church's message of love and sexuality. How many cartoons have managed to find a place even in the minds of the "good little Cathos"! It may be that we—as priests, but also as parents and educators—are not completely strangers to this phenomenon. Obviously, how we present this message greatly affects how it will be received. Between rigor and laxity, ageism and mediocrity, the middle path is not always an easy goal.

The second lesson is a surprise mingled with joy. It is the realization—regardless of the people, their level of religiosity, their standard of living or social status—that there is in all hearts a desire to experience loving for real. I regularly meet young people who are confused by all the logistical guidance on sexuality, who know everything about sex, who have seen everything and even sometimes tried everything, but who seek and who hunger for a sense of meaning, the secret of true joy. They all crave something else! They expect that we dare offer them a kind of ideal that uplifts them and motivates them to excel beyond the "easy stuff." This gives me great hope. Even behind the facade of indifference, even at the bottom of the most wounded hearts, even in spite of major weaknesses, there is a thirst for truth, an intuition that we are all made for a great love that, by itself, can be ultimately fulfilling. Today's youth are even hungering for some guidance that can help them build this love. They want from us adults—priests, parents, educators—that we have the audacity to offer them a way forward—both rigorous and joyful—instead of a false "compassion" that would excuse or legitimize all their mistakes.

That is why I wanted to write this book for you, young people ages fifteen to twenty-two years old. First, because I have a little more experience—I have constantly received your reactions and felt nourished by our always valuable discussions. I therefore wanted to continue adjusting my remarks, improving and deepening my discourse. Writing allows spaciousness, whereas the constraints of a talk can often force one to go too fast. But also because this little book—which I wanted to make readily available—may be passed along or offered to a friend, reread, highlighted or annotated, consulted at your own pace and this, much more easily than with a text found on a computer screen. Many of you asked me to do this or had suggested the idea.

Of course, I am much more at ease when speaking, and I think this book lacks the unique touch that a priest brings to whatever group he is addressing. The written word can never result in the same spontaneity, the smiles and the improvised anecdotes, the moments of laughter or seriousness. But I tried anyway to keep it simple and frank, since these seem to be essential qualities to bring to this topic. Writing this book was an effort for me—I have never been a great writer!—but I am happy to offer it if it can encourage you and enlighten you in your preparations toward real love. I trust in the Lord's fecundity. He is the only infallible master of all love!

Two Precautions

As I begin this writing, I would like to ask your permission that I speak to you frankly. Love, emotional life, sexuality, and friendship are topics too valuable and too important to tackle by avoiding the real issues. There have been too many tepid speeches by adults who are afraid of displeasing young people or, worse, who want to "seem young," and they have wreaked too much havoc in our high schools and chaplaincies. You expect a true, honest, direct discourse from your priests and the Church. You will perhaps not always agree, but at least you have a clear marker that allows you to find your bearings.

I would also like to tell you frankly about a student I remember from my first year of ministry who came to see me after hearing me speak on this issue: a youth like many others, about twenty years old, and who in the arena of love and sex had "some" experience. I can still hear him say, "For six years I was involved with a chaplaincy. Why didn't anyone ever say this to me before? I could have avoided so much damage, both for myself and for a number of people." The heart of a priest cannot remain indifferent to such regrets. Essentially this is my fear as a priest, that I one day cross paths with a boy or girl who tells me, "I had you as a chaplain, vicar, priest . . . and I messed up because you did not dare to be frank with me." In order for this to never happen, I want to talk with humility and frankness.

I want to do this for you because at the same time, I am setting you free. This is the second condition. The purpose of these words is not to give you "recipes" to follow slavishly but to nourish your discernment and to stimulate your thinking. Maybe you will not agree with everything I write. But I want to share with you freely what the heart of a priest wants to tell you about this great theme of love. I do this by drawing on the many lectures I gave on the subject to pupils or students in parishes or schools, and on the often deep exchanges they inspired. My thinking has also been fueled by long discussions with the young people who I was and am able to support, but also by the many testimonies received through social networks or through mail from readers of Padre-blog. I am indebted also to my fellow priests, those who formed me and gave me the urge to preach about the beauty of true love. I must especially sing the praises of the one to whom I owe so much in this area: Father François Potez, a priest with a father's heart who inspired me so much.

Although they are enlightened by the Gospel and the Magisterium of the Church, these are personal insights that I offer. You are free to keep what you want. I am speaking freely precisely because I want to leave you free to choose. All I ask is that you find the humility to let yourself be a little surprised, if not shaken. Please read to the end, and take the time to come back so you can discern, beyond mere agreements or disagreements, what you have kept and why.

Finally, it might be useful to note that these lines are aimed particularly at fifteen- to twenty-year-olds . . . all the way up to maybe twenty-two years for some. Why? Not because this is the age for making significant life choices, but because it is a time for laying foundations. We should write a sequel for those who will make a definitive choice in the short or medium term, for the purpose of clarifying the criteria of discernment and the sense of engagement. Beginning around twenty-three to twenty-four years old, young people are clearly thinking from this perspective; they know in their hearts that the story that is unfolding could lead them to a final commitment that no longer seems so distant. We should be careful not to set age delimitations that are too rigid; all this depends on each person's maturity. Let me just say that my interest is mainly in this period of laying foundations, when it is likely too early to fully engage in love but that the desire to love is already there.

Two Misconceptions

When a priest is called to speak about love and sexuality, one must always start by contesting two challenging ideas that continue to do much harm. Many people, including some of the most Catholic of young people, seem to have these assumptions in mind.

The first misconception is that on the topic of love and sex, all the Church has to offer is a long list of prohibitions. One only needs to look at the expression on high school seniors' faces when the school's principal announces that a priest is coming to give a talk on sexuality! Obviously they might get to avoid two hours of math, but that does not prevent them from sighing at least internally, "He will surely tell us not to have sex before getting married!" This is indeed, for the vast majority of people, the complete message of the Church on love, summarized succinctly as "You are not allowed to sleep together before the wedding!"

I am not exaggerating. There is nothing more destructive than this cliché of a Church that would only propose a list of prohibitions, like a bunch of highway codes of love and sex: "That is sin, that is sin, that too is sin . . . that, you have the right . . . but that is sin." There are no encouraging prospects, only red lines not to cross or sins not to commit. It is awful! A chastity that is made only of frustration and boredom is untenable. A morality that points only to limitations is daunting—perhaps even exhausting. Moreover, experience has shown that these limitations will be broken anyway. A priest who would only limit people would not be teaching anything. "Father, how far can I go with my girlfriend without it being a serious sin?" or "Reverend, is foreplay prohibited?" and so forth. Such questions as these clearly reveal the limits of reducing things to what is allowed or forbidden without first conveying a sense of how love can be engendered or how happiness is at stake. It is all in the service of some happiness. And when the Church wants to teach us how to say no, it is always for the purpose of being able to say yes. We first need to talk about this yes. It will give meaning to all the efforts that will be required. Admittedly, my brother priests and myself should probably ask forgiveness for not always providing this knowledge.

The other misconception is that regarding this topic, the Church would actually be . . . reluctant. And the priests would only be on the defensive, their sole aim being to help avoid or stop the sins that the young people who are under their wing might commit. Worse yet, we think these priests are disconnected. They are "nice," these priests. But in fact they know nothing. They cannot understand. They are simply there to make us respect theoretical rules that seem incredibly far from reality.

There is something quite telling when a guy or girl comes to me to confide that they are in love. My guess is, they are really expecting to be reproached. Yet if they are coming to confide in me, it must be that they trust me. But even then, there is a tendency to be convinced that at first glance the priest will be judging or condemning. At the very least, they will be given a warning: "Be careful! It's sinful!" Besides, most young people only bring up these questions in the confessional. It is terrible to think that subconsciously, such a beautiful theme as love is first and foremost approached in terms of a sin. Sex is only talked about when there is a "slippage" of some kind or there are personal battles for purity. It is so simplistic and, again, it is often deeply discouraging.

A Primarily Positive Perspective

Actually, nothing about these two preconceived ideas is further from the truth regarding the Church's message. It makes me wonder if this is not a first victory of the Devil: to succeed in confusing the beautiful and grand Christian message of human love for a simple discouraging list of prohibitions and thus feed into young people's despair.

When a youth tells me, "I'm in love, I'm in love," my first reaction is to answer, "That's great!" and to rejoice. It is great because you are made for this: to love and be loved. This ability to love is the most beautiful gift that God gave you. That is why the Church's first take on your desire to love is a look of amazement. It is at the heart of God's plan. Open your Bible and read the first pages, the story of Genesis: "God made man for woman, woman for man. . . . Together they shall become one. . . . And God saw that it was good."[3] Nowhere does it say, "God was embarrassed" or "God felt compelled to do that for the reproduction of the species but thought it was dirty." No! "God saw that it was good." What God has placed in the human heart is beautiful and grand. Our ability to love, our thirst for love and for giving of ourselves, is significant and beautiful. The Church marvels at and welcomes this with joy.

Also, the Church loves you too much to lie to you. This capacity for love is both what is most beautiful in you and what is most fragile. The proof lies in the fact that through love, you can make someone the happiest in the world and you yourself can be the happiest in the world. But it is also in this domain of emotional life, of sexuality and of love, that you can hurt yourself the most—and hurt someone else the most as well. Why? Because since the original sin, our hearts are wounded. We thirst for true happiness; we are so happy to be able to achieve this by loving. But this quest is difficult: We end up experiencing our fragility and our ability to hurt others. We experience our egoism as it messes with our finest aspirations. We experience how difficult it is to be discerning and how easy it is to be self-justifying. In fact, we are all so poor in love.

This is why the Church is so demanding, not to prohibit love or even to prevent us from loving. The message of the Church, which is the whole idea behind this book, is twofold: to enhance and to protect our capacity for love. The Church wants us to help make this capacity for love a locus of true joy and not of injury. Because the Church is full of wonder and because it understands this desire for love, it wants to accompany and encourage us while still knowing our frailty. It is therefore with a positive attitude that these subsequent chapters should be read. The Church's joy is to teach us poor ones to love. The joy of the Church is to be of service to our true happiness—a lasting, exigent, full happiness, the happiness of a love that can fill our hearts.

One last point: I ask in advance for your forgiveness if you sometimes feel judged by my words. I would love to first take the time to listen to each of you and to get to know you better before I share these beliefs with you. On this subject, nothing can replace the real and personal connection, the long discussions where the priest can reconcile listening and giving advice, kindness and candor, compassion and exigency. This little book cannot meet everyone's needs. Some may have the impression that I am sometimes too fast, too general, or too opinionated. You might feel judged or injured. This is not my intention. Only God knows your heart and your story. All I can offer you are criteria for discernment so you can judge your actions and distinguish between those who want to build and those who want to destroy. But it is important never to judge someone only for his actions or for his past. We are always worth more than what we did, thankfully. This is what God reveals to us. And this is also why no one should end up feeling discouraged. It is always possible to learn to love.

Learning to Love

In this book you will not find "recipes"—as if the great mystery of love could win prizes—nor lecture courses—as if you could circumnavigate this whole mystery in a few pages. I would instead like to share a few convictions and intuitions that you can later turn to on your own.

Sincerity and Truth

The first intuition is an encouragement; that is, to clearly and promptly make a distinction between "sincerity" and "truth."

Our society is being ruled by sincerity. It is often the sole criterion for declaring that what we do is good: "If it's sincere, then . . ." Every week, young people ask me, "But, Father, why can't we go out together? Why can't we sleep together . . . since, after all, we're being sincere?"

Nevertheless, young people also come to me every week with tears in their eyes, saying, "But, Father, why is it so painful? I was being sincere!" It must indeed be said: you can actually "sincerely" go wrong.

Still, in my experience, many are usually satisfied with their feeling of sincerity when they justify going any further. For example, the vast majority of youth agree that a slightly indecent "nab" for one evening is not very honorable. One ends up feeling neither embarrassed nor proud. But as soon as a little sincerity is invoked, everything seems to be justifiable.

It reminds me of the story of this boy, a nineteen-year-old student who came to see me after the World Youth Day (WYD) in Cologne in 2005. (I also want to add, in jest: Those WYDs are great! They have had an effect on the emotional life of more than one of you!) This young man told me that he is going out with this girl with whom he is very much in love. My initial reaction was to say, "That's great!" I then said, "Please tell me—explain to me why you chose her."

Here is what he told me:

"I met her at WYD."

"But when did you start dating her?"

"Well . . . since WYD!" (The WYD is five days long, or up to ten days for the extended version.)

"I see, anyway . . . that's rather fast. How did you choose her?"

"We didn't know each other, but our respective groups of friends found themselves in the same bus. We met there and we instantly made a strong bond. During the next few days, we talked, we shared things, and we discussed lots. I was really into her. So it happened at the final vigil with the pope."

"Ah . . . the vigil with the pope. (Note that two million young people are gathered for hours in the sun, and then in the heat of the night, two million small candles, the songs . . . the very "cozy" atmosphere, which is all actually quite seductive.) Tell me."

"Well, we had a really great evening, feeling a strong bond, sitting side by side. In my heart I really felt that it was her, that I had to tell her. I was thoroughly into her. I never prayed like that before. I felt that something was happening. At the end, we said the Rosary together, pressed against each other . . . and suddenly, at the end of the Rosary . . . well, it happened!"

I was thus discovering some of the effects of the Rosary. This boy was being totally sincere. He did not "nab" his sweetheart in a contemptible way, just for a night or to take advantage of her. But his judgment was minimized, both in time (five days!) and in substance: "I felt," "It was strong," and so forth. This cannot be enough to create a solid, lasting relationship.

In truth, sincerity alone is not enough to engender the actions and words that demonstrate love. For these gestures and words to build happiness and love, we must respect their innate truth: not just what they mean to us, but also the meaning they objectively carry within them. As a Christian I would say, "The sense that God gave them." When it comes to learning to love, it will not suffice to say, "For me, I think that . . ." or "The Church says that, but I think that. . . ." Is this not the ideal area in which we must humbly recognize that we always have something to learn? Is He who gave me the ability to love not the best one to teach me how to love? To reveal to me the sense that He gave these gestures and words of love? To pass on to me the truth behind these gestures and words? Basically, if God wants our happiness, do we not have everything to gain by signing up for his training in love? That is why, for the readers of this book who are Christians, this learning to love cannot be separated from a true spiritual approach. It is because I choose to trust in Christ that I agree to follow his advice and path, for which the Church is the most important voice: "If you knew the gift of God" (John 4:10 NIV).

Loving and Being in Love

In order to appreciate this distinction between sincerity and truth, we need to go a little further to rediscover the difference between "loving" and "being in love." Some will think it is a simple matter of ABCs. Alas, even newlyweds a few months into their marriage do not really understand these things. This young man from the WYD was undoubtedly very much in love, but was he ready to love?

What does it mean to "be in love"? Here we are speaking of feelings and therefore of sincerity. We love when we sincerely feel a mysterious and honest attraction to a person. Let us focus on this feeling and its features.

We must first recognize that we are not completely a free agent with respect to this feeling. It is impossible to master what one feels. So we do not really decide with whom we fall in love or when we will fall in love. This is also what makes this feeling so entrancing. There is something a bit mysterious within it: "Why him?" "Why her?" There is not really a complete, logical, mathematical answer to this question: "Because he is the one!" "Because she is the one!"

That is why it even happens that one can fall in love without having actually decided. A priest who is happy to be a priest can suddenly feel an affinity that turns into feelings of love for a beautiful and devoted parishioner. This is the reason why he cultivates some caution in order not to promote the emergence of such a feeling. A wife or a husband can also "fall" in love with another man or woman. The very expression "falling in love" points to the fact that we cannot totally master the feelings that can spring from our heart. This should not surprise us. The real question is, how do we manage that feeling when it springs up?

If we cannot control what we feel, the feeling of love can, therefore, also fluctuate a lot.

We can, for instance, be genuinely in love with someone for six months and then recognize with the same sincerity that after six months we find ourselves ultimately attracted to another person. I have known some young people who are genuinely in love with a different person every three weeks!

We may well be in love with several different people in our lives. We do not necessarily fall in love with the person who will be our spouse on the first try.

One can sincerely be in love after five days of WYD, after two hours of an evening together, or during a summer vacation. Or, conversely, love can grow out of the experience of a long and slow maturation with a feeling that takes its time to hatch.

Initially the feeling of love is often a mixed bag. There is a need for affection: the desire to love and to be loved pushes us into the arms of another. There is also sometimes a fear of being alone. But let's face it, there can also be some selfishness underneath it all: one loves the other for what they bring, not for who they are. In its early stages, the feeling of love is often very idealistic: We can be dazzled by the ideal image we have created of the beloved. We do not see this person as they are but more as we imagine them to be. We do not yet appreciate their limitations and their faults. At first, this is quite normal. And it is good to just be aware.

This feeling of love, is it wrong? Certainly not. It is definitely something beautiful that one should not try to repress—except when it conflicts with our loyalty to the life choices we have made. The feeling of love is even the first normal and necessary step in building a lasting love. Everything usually starts with the attraction and desire that have made so many poets, writers, and artists express themselves, starting with the author of the Song of Songs. (By the way, this is a good source of inspiration for all lovers who do not know what to write to their beloved.)

It is important to cultivate this feeling of love throughout our lives. I often say to married couples: Stay in love! Cultivate this game of love like in the early days of your relationship. Blessed are those who—having become parents—remain spouses while keeping a betrothed's heart, full of fantasies, surprises, affection, and tenderness.

But still, what is the difference between "loving" and "being in love"? Being in love is a matter of feeling. Loving is about the will to freely commit. To love is to choose to love, to want to love.

On the day of your wedding at city hall or at the church, the mayor or the priest will not ask if you are "in love," or if you want him or her, or what you "feel" toward this person, because you cannot simply promise to feel the same yearning every day, twenty-four hours a day, seven days a week. We cannot master this desire. Even for the most faithful couples, the feeling of love has its ups and downs. When we return from work after a good scolding from the boss and an hour of traffic jams, and we find an empty fridge, a temperamental child at a difficult age and with a bad report card to sign, and then we learn moreover that the stepmother has arrived three days early . . . at that moment it is hard to have loving feelings. We might only feel like walking out the door. Does this mean that we no longer love our partner? No! We want to love them. Beyond what we feel, we choose to love again and again.

That is why the priest or the mayor will ask you this question instead: "Do you choose to. . . ?" We cannot promise to feel a burning desire every day of our lives. But we can promise our beloved that we want to love them every day of our lives. And this is indeed something magnificent: beyond the more or less burning sentiment, we still have our freedom, that is, the ability to choose to love.

Of course, it is easier to want to love when the desire is present. That is why it is important to cultivate it. But the commitment will not rest simply on this desire. It will also rely on free will. Love requires the engagement of the will. "Yes, I want this." How beautiful it is to see a young person able to engage their whole life with a "Yes, I want this." What a joy to hear the one we love say, before God and all people, "I choose you." Knowing that desire sometimes fluctuates, we also know that when we have our beloved's word expressing something more than just desire, it helps us engage ourselves and confidently offer ourselves.

This is also why loyalty is possible. Contrary to what we often think, marriage does not shelter one from having feelings or an attraction for someone else. But it is important to understand that beyond what we can feel one day, there is freedom. We are not necessarily responsible for the nascent desires within us—unless we have worked really hard to make them come alive—but we are responsible for our response. We can choose not to feed this desire, to distance ourselves from its cultivation and from allowing it to take root. We can also renew our choice to love the one we have chosen. We will do everything we can to awaken or reanimate the feeling of love that was our initial intention.

Maybe you now understand a little better one of the essential objectives of emotional intelligence: to learn to grow one's feelings and desires instead of repressing them. There is nothing inherently wrong with sexual desire. God has created it and God does not want to cause harm. It should not be the intention of Christianism to frustrate us into repressing all desire. Christianism wants for us to be creatures of desire and especially free agents. We are free because we are masters of our own selves, able to be at the helm in our lives without being tyrants about it. This is indeed one of the key elements of the struggle for purity, a particularly difficult struggle for boys approaching the age of maturity. But it is important to be conscious of this struggle in order to understand what is at stake. It is indeed about gradually learning to master one's desires, to bring them in line with one's personal dedication. We need for the body to be of service and for the heart and mind to lead the way. This is the objective of a long journey for all of us.

The difference between "a feeling of love" and "love" is thus made more clear. We can "fall in love" suddenly or within a few days, but to choose to be in love necessitates knowledge. To know someone to the point of choosing them requires time. We can also experience the fluctuations in the feeling of love, but when we make a willful choice, love will be stable and lasting if we have given it time to mature. When I say that to love is to choose, I see that within the expression of "choice" there are the notions of engagement and duration. We can be in love with or attracted to the somewhat ideal image of the person, or we can be drawn to what that person can bring us. But we cannot choose someone solely based on who they are or how they really are with their particular qualities and limitations.

What can we conclude out of this?

The conclusion is something quite simple but essential: to go from "I'm in love" to "I love," time is of the essence. This lapse of time is what allows discernment so we can go from a simple desire to an engaged choice. This time of discernment is often missing within incidental encounters; it can also be lacking in a longer-lasting relationship when the couple finds itself compromised.

Injuries

Why do so many young people end up feeling hurt?

Because many of them end up giving into words or deeds (and in my opinion, both are equally important) that say "I love you" when really they are lusting after another.

Let's be clear. It is cool to say "I love you" to someone. It is indeed something beautiful, especially if it is real. Sometimes the feeling is sincere, especially when spending an evening with the object of our desire. It is beautiful if it is real, that is, if it really matches the true meaning of the word—to be clear, if it means,

"I am ready to choose you, to be committed. I want to build a life with you for the duration."

The next time someone tells you "I love you," ask them to be specific. The word *love* has too much weight to risk being misled or to risk misleading someone. "What does that mean for you? You want me? You're sincerely in love? Just as you were many times before? Just as you could be again? Or are you ready to partner with me for the duration? Are you saying this after a long maturation of your feelings, after having experienced your feelings, after taking the time to know me, to understand me as I am and for who I am? Among all the ones with whom you've been in love or with whom you could be in love, you decided to choose me?" You should understand that an "I love you" cannot allow any ambiguity, unless it is lacking in its true meaning and its veracity.

It is certainly not a sin to go out with someone, in the sense of making a life together and moving forward toward discernment. To kiss, in and of itself, is not a bad thing. It is even cool, and it is an important step in the process. Of course, you will not marry someone you met last night. There will naturally be a time of companionship and of discernment accompanied by natural moments of tenderness. Still, the words and deeds of love cannot be made simple. Indeed, they engage us fully if we respect their veracity and if we do not consider them to be nonsense. Kissing is already a step toward giving of oneself. It is the first step toward a total offering of oneself and a promise of a more significant engagement. This can only be accomplished if in our hearts we are ready to make that promise, if we are ready to take the next step toward this commitment and this total offering of oneself, and if we are at home in this way of being.

Many people end up being happy to "be together" or basically "in love" enough to start going out and to begin a relationship. This is not fundamentally a "sin"; it is mostly trivial. We are engaging in a relationship that will affect us one way or another without really having made a choice. On the one hand, we find ourselves mostly free: "We're good together. We'll have to see what the future will hold, but for the moment, we don't talk about it much." On the other hand, we are engaged in deeds that affect us. We become more emotionally involved. When it all comes to a head, the discrepancy between these opposites becomes the source of great suffering.

I do not mean to say that the only girl or the only boy with whom you will go out will necessarily have to be your future wife or husband. There are obviously serious relationships that end up nowhere, indeed because you have taken the time to make an important discernment. There are also engagements that are broken. It can be seriously painful, but it will not cause any harm if both parties have not taken this lightheartedly. Each person made an effort to discern, to make space for the idea that they each would last for the duration. Each took the time to build upon a personal discernment that allowed each to conclude that a journey together would make it possible to go further.

Paradoxically, what is most troublesome in my opinion are those incidental encounters, those relationships that do not last long because they have not been thought through very carefully. "We were feeling drawn to each other. We had some feelings. We got together rapidly or felt pushed into it by some momentary desire. And we lasted as long as we were

OK together, until the day we both admitted to each other that we were no longer feeling drawn; we no longer felt anything. Our feelings for each other had changed. We went out together for six months, a year, two years . . . and then, pretty quickly, we got together with someone else. We gave of ourselves without really taking the time to choose to commit."

Sexual relations . . . they are also very cool. Is it not great to be able to express the gift of the heart with the gift of the body? Is it not great to do it with the shared joy and intense pleasure resulting from a very specific kind of communion between spouses and not from some kind of "mastered" technique? The Church does not have any problems with sex. On the contrary, it finds these sexual relations to be so beautiful that it wants to protect their full meaning and their authenticity.

The authenticity of the sexual act is that it is an expression of an exclusive and definite love. It expresses a complete offering of one's person for the love of another. This offering is engaging: it affects the person on all levels; it creates a very strong physical bond that reveals and expresses to the one we love a definite yes that cannot be taken back. Many engage in these sexual relations in a sincere way without ultimately waiting to be in a decisive commitment. But in this way this act inevitably loses its full meaning, its radicalness, and its power. It no longer carries the certainty of a definitive offering.

A twenty-year-old man told me he finally understood this, although a little late. He had just been "rejected" by his girlfriend after a relationship of about one year. They had engaged in sexual relations, persuaded that they were really ready and convinced that each was the other's first and only lover: "You see, Father, I now understand why you asked me to wait before giving of myself. I can erase all the exchanged emails. I can delete all the text messages. I can throw away all the letters. But I can't rid myself of the fact that I gave myself over completely. Unfortunately, we really weren't ready for this kind of relationship." Even if God's mercy can, fortunately, forgive and repair many things, we remain marked by these engaging relationships.

You might want to say, "My dear Father, you are under some kind of spell! People have been easily drawn to kissing, going out, or sleeping together for a long time. You need to face reality! Even for Cathos!"

Be reassured, any priest who offers confession is not under some kind of spell. He is seeing things for what they are. The Church has accompanied men and women for two thousand years. This gives it a certain experience of the greatness and of the misery of the human heart. Therefore why should you be attentive to what I am telling you? Why encourage you to wait and keep to yourself? Is the battle not already lost from the get-go? Is this not an inaccessible ideal?

No, I do not think so. I even believe otherwise.

The Real Challenge

The challenge must not be to only avoid sin. When chastity is reduced to crossing a red line, it cannot survive. Even if we are told "It's a sin," experience has shown us that this is not enough. We must have a good reason to be demanding of ourselves.

The real challenge is to prepare ourselves to be the husband or wife we want to someday be.

If today you become acclimated to engaging in these acts of love too quickly, too soon, too easily, without allowing them all their meaning, you risk debasing them. You will miss being able to turn to them when you finally are ready to love. When the one you truly love asks you, "Tell me, when you kiss me, what does it mean to you?" You will answer, "It means that I love you very much."

"OK, but then, with the last person, what did it mean?"

"Ah, well, that was different. It didn't mean anything! You're the first one for whom I feel this strongly, whom I love this much."

How not to think, "Yes, but you also said this to the last person in relation to the one before that. You must have said it at least twenty times by now! How can I trust you? How can I rely on your words and your deeds and in turn give of myself if I know that you offered these words and deeds so many times before? You have given them away so easily. How can I be certain that this time it will be lasting and true?"

Therein lies the question that the Church is asking of you: "What are you keeping for the one you will truly love one day? What are you learning to hold for that special one? Do they deserve that you wait for them?"

Many have argued, "Father, I concur with building a home life at the age of twenty-five to thirty years old. Please believe me, at that moment, I'll be mindful. But for now, between the ages of fifteen to twenty-five, let us do what we want in peace! We want to be able to discover things without losing our minds over it." Only you are now under a spell. I have prepared many couples for marriage, and I can promise you one thing: things do not change easily on the eve of our wedding! It is not on the eve of our wedding that we learn fidelity. It is not on the eve of our wedding that we learn to say no in order to better hold on to our yes. And it is not on the eve of our wedding that we learn self-mastery. No. On the eve of our wedding, we are the result of the ten years that have come before. What you are living between the ages of fifteen and twenty will mark you deeply and will lead to your future.

This is also a truth that the Church cannot hide, because the Church loves you: it is not at age twenty-five that one prepares for marriage. It is at fifteen years old. This is not because at fifteen you have already discovered your future wife or husband, but rather because ·what you are experiencing at age fifteen and beyond prepares you for being the husband or wife you will be at age twenty-five or thirty.

I came to understand this much better during one of the first weddings I officiated. A young couple had wanted to connect very seriously with each other without being too significantly influenced by their group of friends. They had taken their time before going out with each other, then they took it slowly before getting engaged. They had also wanted to experience a real engagement, deciding to wait until they were married to offer themselves to each other. None of this was really easy for them, and it was not really understood by their friends. They had the impression they were like *The Last of the Mohicans*, but they held on to their convictions. They were no stronger than anyone else. They had some challenges along the way, but they took it all in stride, taking it all as a gift for each other.

The day of their wedding, I noticed two significant things. First, their joy was palpable. Imagine the joy of a twenty-four-year-old fiancée who hears her fiancé tell her, "You know, it was sometimes really hard, but for me, I learned to wait, I learned to contain myself, and I learned to pick myself back up." She knows what kinds of effort this represents these days. She understands the weight of his words. And imagine the fiancé's joy when he hears the one who loves him say, "You know, I wanted to learn to save these moments for you, even before I knew you. I learned to wait for you. I kept myself for you." I can assure you that this sustained their joy. They experienced their shared efforts as symbolic of their love; greed had no place here. They were too humble, too fragile, to let any such feeling take over. And they were not perfect in any way, but they demonstrated a joy so clear when it came time to harvest the fruits of their efforts.

The second thing that I noticed was the look of envy—in the noble sense of the word— among their friends. One of them came to see me during the reception. I will never forget what he confided in me. He must have been twenty-five years old. He was a kind young man, but he had not chosen the same path at all. One could almost say that he had an impressive "score card." He told me, "You know, Father, when I see the joy in both of them, I finally understand what they were trying to accomplish. We made fun of them lots, for sure. But this evening, I would sure like to trade places with them. Unfortunately I'm not sure if I'm capable of that same joy. I gave of myself too much."

This young man's revelation shocked me. Here is a man with a lot of strength, able to accomplish many things, but who finds himself doubting his ability to love, to be loyal, to know this happiness "because he gave of himself too much." Why was there no one at his side when he was sixteen, eighteen, or twenty years old, asking him, "What are you keeping for the one you will one day love?"

The challenge is an important one. It is nothing short of preparing for the joy we want to offer and the joy we want to have when the time comes and we are ready to offer ourselves to someone. There are some real questions to ask ourselves: "What kind of joy do I want to be capable of? What kind of joy do I want to offer the one I will love?"

Some will say that all this will be scary for people. What do we say about those who indeed have already fallen, who are already somewhat hurt, or very much so? I will come back to this. Thankfully God's mercy is already at work. One thing is for sure: it is much easier to change habits at age sixteen than eighteen, at eighteen than twenty-five, and at twenty-five than thirty. There is always the possibility to pick oneself back up. There is always time to learn to love. But the more we have gotten involved in easy connections, the more effort it will take to pick ourselves back up. That is why the Church does not mind honestly address-ing these issues with young people as of the age of fifteen.

This conversation is not intended to scare people away. Its intention is to incite respon-sibility. It is true, what you are living today affects how you will be tomorrow. Is this not the most incredible motivator? Of course, the mistakes, the stupidities, the errors you have committed in this area can sometimes mark you for a long time. But the reverse is also true: all the good deeds you are accomplishing and all of the truthful living you are doing prepares you positively for the future husband or wife you will be.

That is why this message is enlivening when we grasp it. It is in order to point you toward the promised day that the Church invites you to free yourself of what is not completely true or what is too easy. It is in order to be able to say yes one day that the Church encourages you to sometimes say no. Your efforts, your understanding of this inner freedom, your battle for purity, your exigency—all prepare you for the joy of yes. That is the treasure you will get to offer your beloved. It is for him or her that you are already giving the best of yourself, that you are fighting for what is right, that you want to keep your clarity—even if you do not know him or her yet.

Of course, it is impossible to land here all at once. It is about a state of mind. Those who do not care today will be crying tomorrow. And those who cry today—because it is often considered rude to get back up and to learn to say no, or to renounce to one thing or another, or to struggle against discouragement—will be laughing and giving thanks tomorrow. It is not about being perfect all at once. We all learn to love step-by-step, from recovery to recovery. It is simply about learning to love for real.

When we go for a run in the mountains, the most decisive moment is paradoxically at the beginning: the choice of which summit to climb. We have a choice between a number of peaks. There is the 2,600-foot one that is not too high, not too hard. The great majority go there and are happy with their decision. After all, it is really not too bad compared with the 1,000-foot hill, not the mention the crevasse! And then there is the 10,000-foot summit. On this one, the path is steeper. It is hard to get to it in one fell swoop; we might fall flat on our face and get back up. Fewer people dare to venture up this one. It is too hard and too long. But those who have explored the mountains know the joy of having climbed 10,000 feet does not compare with the joy of having climbed 2,600 feet.

We are made for the joy of reaching 10,000 feet! We are made for the joy of great love, which is the fruit of a long and sometimes laborious preparation. "We pay for joy first, then we pay for pleasure," as Father Potez often says.[1] Joy is experienced on the mountain: the joy of reaching the summit comes from the effort of the climb. But those who do not care about this risk regretting it one day. Between fifteen and twenty years old, that is the age of choosing the summit. No one is asking you to get there immediately—and easily! But the Church is asking you to not be easily satisfied. It encourages you to not be satisfied with incidental encounters that follow one another and that do not compare with the great love for which you were made. It wants to give you a taste of the summit and to convince you that everyone is able to get there.

Priests offer their lives to lead you there: letting you do it at your own pace, without doing it for you, and helping you get up when you fall. And they will remind you, day in and day out, that you were made for the summit; that is where your joy will be. On their way, and with the idea in mind that each step gets them closer to the summit, the climber gets a taste of this joy. They know that a great happiness awaits them. The same goes for you. This arduous and meaningful journey will be a journey of happiness. The Church's message is not meant to be a set of shackles under which you are left saddened or crushed. It is a joyful journey—authentically joyful: each small victory, each time you get back up, prepares you for the greatest love.

Many complain about the Church's discourse on this matter. They accuse it of being square, of making young people run away because of its high demands, because of being out of sync. I want to nonetheless ask you this question: Who respects you the most? Those who want to easily please you by offering the following words: "Go for it . . . it's common at your age . . . have fun . . . have your experiences . . . stay safe but abandon yourself to the process"? Or those who want the best for you and are willing to let you know about it? The pope could also offer a similar, easy discourse just to please the media. That would be dramatic! It would in fact mean that he no longer believes in your ability to prepare yourselves for real love. But the pope will never treat you this way. He prefers taking a hit and letting himself be insulted by the "opinion makers" and other lowly stars of politics and the media whose capacity for love is so worn they would rather disenfranchise you as well. He prefers seeming square rather than lying to you.

The Church is like a mother: It loves you too much to lie to you. It does not lie about the objective it has in mind for you. And it accompanies you along your journey. It will help you get back up as many times as you need. It will never leave you halfway through. Whatever the errors and mistakes you have made in the past, it calls upon you never to let go, never to feel discouraged, because all of us were made for real love.

Three Useful Sayings

All this is nice. But is it possible? Whether you are Christian or not, you all aspire to this great love in your heart. One day, after a talk I gave, some young high school girls came to see me. They wanted to talk. At first they were quite antagonistic . . . because they had experienced certain things. Often, they had these experiences with older boys. They gave the impression of having seen it all, having tried it all, and being on top of it all. They had offered themselves quite often, and they took it really hard that I considered this to be a problem. They sought reassurance by questioning everything they thought I had said. As our exchange proceeded, their veneer started to break. I ended up asking one of them this question: "Tell me, really: What is your dream, if anything were possible?"

"I want to meet a boy who loves me and respects me. I'd like to have a family with him!"

In one sentence she stated what she had never experienced but that she always hoped for. Yes, in spite of it all, she was dreaming of that great love. Nonetheless, she did not think it would be possible. "It doesn't exist!" or "It's too late!" Thus she tried to persuade herself that going from one relationship to another would suffice in filling her heart. In order to find the tenderness she so desired, she gave it all and gave herself—to the point of not believing in it.

The Church knows our hearts. Even under a mountain of wounds and mistakes there lives a desire for what is true: a thirst for loving and being loved. It would be terribly cruel on God's part to create this desire in us and make it impossible to achieve. "It's big, yes, but it's hard!" "It's so contrary to everything!" How many times have I heard these regrets? Let me offer you three concrete ways to help you move forward. These are three simple sayings that you can keep and meditate on. I am borrowing them once again from Father François Potez, while expanding upon them with my own words.

Not Too Soon!

There is a time for everything.

First, there is a time to create oneself before creating something in a couple. How could you create something solid together without first having created yourself?

You can sincerely be in love at age fifteen, eighteen, or twenty. That is pretty good! But are you ready to love, that is, to choose another at that age? Though it might seem straightforward, you are not yet fully formed at that age, and the other person is not yet the man or woman you think you might be choosing. That is expected. You are in love at that age? OK, then keep that somewhere inside your heart and let it ripen. Then do your best to become the person you want someone to love. Take the time to build yourself, to take your studies seriously—boys are especially challenged with being good at doing two things at the same time! Take time to strengthen your character, to develop your personality, to grow your capacity for commitment by being faithful to those you have already chosen—Scouting, chaplaincy, fraternity, and so forth. Intensify your prayer life, exercise your will, learn self-control. In short, prepare the strong man and woman you will soon offer over to love. The one you are secretly in love with will thank you. That special person needs a woman or a man who is solid and formed, capable of committing themselves. When you decide to reveal yourself, your special one will be able to understand that this is not the overly generous expression of a fragile teenage desire but the mature and proven intention of a free-thinking man or woman.

I think again about this twenty-year-old man who came to complain to me. He could never feel secure, going from one girl to the next, always in love with a new one. I asked him, "Since you were fourteen or fifteen years old, how long have you been alone?"

"At most, four months!"

"That's your problem, my friend. You never had the opportunity to learn to be strong for yourself. You've always needed an emotional crutch. Take the time to form yourself. You'll then be able to love a girl, not for what she brings you but for who she is, primarily."

Not too soon! The high school years, the start of the student years, are there for you to form and train yourself. Many do not take advantage of these years, remaining prisoners of their repeated heartaches or of an all-too-passionate affair. I see too many young couples who seem to be like old married couples. At twenty years old, some are already going out on a weekend for two or even a weeklong "couples" holiday abroad. What will be left for them to discover once they are married? How sad it is to see young people as young as eighteen, glued to each other, unable to leave each other in peace, prisoners of their daily dose of text messages. Their friends keep complaining. They say, "We no longer get to see him without his girlfriend!" I think back to this eighteen-year-old guy who told me, somewhat sheepishly, that he was texting his "girlfriend" one hundred times per day. Every night they called each other and spoke for more than an hour to "fall asleep together." This happened nightly! And he could not wait to reconnect with her every weekend. What an enmeshed and stuffy relationship! How could one believe for a moment that it could last a long time without any problems?

Ah, these terms: "My boyfriend," "my girlfriend." It is cute . . . but it is awful. Why do you say she is "yours"? Does she belong to you? What are you committed to? You were with another girl six months earlier, and you will be with yet another in a year. And then, why "friend"? It is very cute, the friendly couples out of high school who give each other friendly pecks before sending friendly text messages and calling each other for an hour each evening when unlimited calling is available. It is cute, but that is precisely all it is: it is friendly.[1]

Note that I do not consider any of this sinful. All this can be very chaste, but it is very hard to keep it this way for years. I will return to this. But these are "short stories," as they say. But you are not made for "short stories." You are made for the great love. You are not made for boyfriends and girlfriends; you are made to live great friendships. The high school age is not the time of girlfriends and boyfriends. It is the time of good friends, of what is most beautiful in friendship, what is more liberating and more constructive. It is the time of manly friendships between guys and deep friendships between girls; these beautiful, inspiring friendships within your groups of boy or girl friends, friendships that will fulfill you and take away the draw toward those disappointing piddly affairs.

Not too soon—that means, do not "zap" this time of friendship. You are in love with that boy? Very good. Do not make him your boyfriend. Instead, consider him to be one of your good friends within a wider group of friends. You noticed this girl? Very good. Start by building a friendship with her. Why? Because this time of good friendships is precious; it is not wasted time. The best way to get to know the one with whom you are going to be in love is precisely through this group of friends. In a group, each person reveals their truth. We learn to know each other freely because friendship is not exclusive. We do not isolate ourselves too soon or too fast in a seductive relationship or in a couple. Friendship is free; it purifies what may be selfish in the initial rush to love. Friendship asks nothing and imposes nothing. It teaches freely.

One day, of course, this particular affection will become explicit. You will have to take the plunge and expose yourselves. In fact, there is no specific age for this. It all depends on the maturity of each person. However, experience shows that the encounters that are started very early are either easy to construct nor easy to live with peacefully and clearly. Why? Because if you start going out at age sixteen or eighteen, but you cannot get married until you are twenty-four or twenty-five, you will find that time passes by very slowly. The wait will be difficult, and you might have the impression that you are running in place. The heart and mind will often understand that time is of the essence (it is hard to imagine being married at sixteen . . . hardly anyone wants to think about it), but the body can be very eager to go all the way. Your desires can be powerful at any age. It will require a kind of bravery to live all of those years while holding the same ideal.

My experience as a confessor has shown me that it is quite unusual. One time, I attended a wedding for a couple who had been dating since the ages of fourteen and fifteen. I told them they were surprising me a little by offering a beautiful counterexample of what I always said in my lectures. They laughed and reassured me that, "On the contrary, the fact of being together so early did not at all facilitate our capacity for discernment. When we were fifteen, we would have liked to come across a priest who could have told us to let go of each other a bit and to take our time!" They pointed out the inherent challenge: How can one discern when one is so young? Indeed, the steps that you take early in life may create pathways that are not in service to freedom and discernment when you are ready for them.

I think back to those girls. There were three of them, in tenth grade or so, though one would easily add five more years to their age as is often the case in the institutions of these beautiful Parisian neighborhoods. They were magnificent young girls, very comfortable in their skin. At the end of the conference, they came to see me, being quite affected by what they had heard. They were all going out with boys.

The first one began, "Father, I liked what you said, so I want to ask your advice. Well, me and my boyfriend, I feel we have communication problems as a couple. It's hard for us to take time to listen to each other; it's difficult to figure out how best to share our thoughts with each other."

The second one chimes in: "For me, it's about the sex. In my relationship with my boyfriend,

I feel that it's hard to really connect. In fact, we're simply not at the same level of desire and I feel that."

I interrupted her. "But wait! Stop! You sound like forty-year-old women who are coming to tell me about your problems with your husbands! You're sixteen! This isn't the time to be worried about these things. You put yourselves in complicated situations only to get yourselves in a can of worms. You find yourselves working through difficulties that are clearly not for your age. Claim your freedom, your carefreeness, your natural selves. Claim the concerns and priorities of your age. Don't miss these years."

Not too soon. As fifteen- to twenty-year-olds, you are invited to dream of discovering the world, to give of yourselves to the simplicity of a scout camp, to share major projects you might accomplish with friends, to open up to each other's richness, to be passionate about particular causes, to cultivate your talents. But you do not need to lock yourselves into a small, comfortable emotional bubble that separates you from others or may cause you to miss these important years.

I am deeply affected by some young people who give the impression that they are already "experienced." They have easily done everything, tried everything, and claim to be very liberated. They have "lived." I sense them to be especially bored and a little indifferent. They are eager to try new experiences because everything seems bland to them. I think back to that seventeen-year-old who told me he was "tired" of the Parisian clubs and the "plan C"! What was left for him to discover? He was "worn out," and so soon. Many young people want to be free. In the end, they are "liberated" but hardly free. Then again, beneath the veneer, how many of them admit that they have become completely dependent on the need to please or to seduce? How many depend on one-night stands to be easily reassured that they know how to "hustle" and get a girl in bed? How many girls find themselves suddenly in need of tenderness at all costs, a need that would make them sacrifice anything, including their purity? How many young people no longer know the simple joy of spending an evening with friends, foregoing all the excesses that are not necessary to spend a good and fun evening?

I am infinitely saddened to witness hearts
that are aged by sin, by addiction, or by habit.
They hide themselves behind finery; they learn
to maintain a reassuring facade for their parents
or for their peers. They would never admit—to
those who see them as a cool party-animal kind
of guy, sure of himself, or as a confident, cool,
and relaxed girl—that they end up often being
disgusted with these endless and hopeless stories,
these drunken parties, and these repeated blun-
ders. Then comes a day when they are recognized
by a true friend, one that asks nothing of them.
Or they reveal themselves in the confidence of a
confession to a priest with a father's heart. What
a relief, then, to finally be true to oneself!

I am not saying you need to be rigid or stuck,
sad or withdrawn. Life is not limited to a binary.
You just need to realize that you are all precious.
And that your capacity to love, your heart, and
your body are infinitely precious. Nothing can
justify the destruction of this truth. This is a
very important issue: to show that one can be
happy, joyful, and open to the world without
this being at the expense of what is beautiful
inside. On the contrary, it is who you are that
must radiate out of you—your ideals, your

beliefs, your greatest desires, your thirst for life—that must make you be the first on the dance floor, or have a nice dinner with friends, or walk in the mountains, or go on a sailboat.

Not too soon . . . to take the time to be anchored in the real joys. To have the time to learn to cultivate one's desire and one's will. Not too soon to allow this time of great friendships to make you a boy or a girl who knows what he or she wants—who is true to what he believes, what she carries within her—and even more open and radiant in the presence of others. Do not let anything or anyone steal this time of youth away from you. Let yourself free each other. Enjoy this time. It is a time of building foundations. A house is strong only if its foundation is solid. We can build the highest wall in the world, but if the foundation is weak, the whole house will remain fragile. Take time to build this foundation, even if you are eager to see the walls go up, the roof cover all this, and the interior get furnished.

Not Too Fast!

Not too fast means to accept that great things cannot be accomplished without taking time.

Those who built cathedrals knew it was the work of a lifetime. Is it not also true of your future home?

Not too fast means to take some time. Take time to appreciate that your romantic feelings will need to grow in order to choose love. That your initial desires will lead to first steps. That the first impetus will become the first confidence. Take time for discernment. Even when the body is impatiently ready and wants satisfaction, the heart and the intelligence, in turn, need time to discern and to grow in peace.

A twenty-one-year-old girl came to have a talk with me. She had just put an end to a four-year relationship with a boy. She said something that struck me: "You know, Father, with X, we immediately fell into mad, passionate love. We quickly gave ourselves to the relationship. We gave it all. We couldn't let go. In the eyes of our friends, we were the perfect couple. I now realize that in those four years we never really chose each other. Our bodies had chosen each other, our need for affection had chosen each other. But we had never taken the time and freedom necessary to fully choose each other."

Not too fast means agreeing to put the brakes on your sensitive desires. Do not worry, they will grow by themselves and very quickly! Take better care of your freedom and respect other people's freedom, for it is by remaining free that you will be able to think through and discern what you feel. If you move too quickly and you get hurt, this will have a significant effect—perhaps even bodily—that you are probably not willing to undertake or that could encroach on your freedom of discernment. How many, for example, try not to ask too many questions for fear of getting lost? They cling to another person while knowing deep down inside that there is very little future in what they are doing. But they are no longer free. They hunger for these signs of tenderness, for the pleasure of the body and the presence of another person, without having actually chosen.

When I hear girls say, "Father, I haven't told him no because I was afraid of losing him if I did not go out with him right away." And they tell me the same a few months later, "Father, I have not told him no because I was afraid of losing him if I did not sleep with him." How can you believe that there is even one gram of love in this relationship? Love imposes nothing. Love asks nothing. Love does not blackmail. Love is exposed, it proposes, it is received. Love knows how to be patient. Love knows how to wait. How can we build a relationship out of fear of getting lost? That is the sign of a lack of freedom. Rest assured, if he really loves you, he will wait for you, and he will build his own foundation in the meantime.

Sleeping with your boyfriend or girlfriend, everyone does it! Unfortunately, this statement has very little value anymore. On the contrary, being able to wait and to hold your love for the one you will choose, so that you will give yourself on the day that you have promised never to turn back—yes! This is an admirable gesture of love of which you are capable. A boy who can wait, or a girl who knows how to restrain herself, or anyone who at least wants to try: that is a good sign. This is not an assurance that he or she is a good person, of course! But this means that at least the other person takes you seriously. He wants to take steps toward discernment. She respects you too much to risk hurting you by removing herself after having given herself.

Not so fast means to remain free. Do not become a repressed person, but learn to cultivate your desire. Everything, right now? No, not in love. We are the generation of immediacy and instant gratification. Give yourself the grace of time and duration. Here again, I hear too many young people say, "Father, we were two good friends, and we went a little fast. We should have waited; we would have understood that we were made to stay friends. But because of what we've been through, it's hard to find that friendship now."

Not so fast means learning to say no in order to better say yes when you are ready. How many young people end up doubting themselves because they never went out with someone at eighteen to twenty years old? Social pressure—and sometimes the pressure of relatives or friends—causes us to acclimate ourselves to fads and habits for fear of appearing "cut off." It is sad. The one we should admire in a class is not the one with the fullest scorecard! This only proves that he is not able to say no. And he will be able to say yes. The one we should admire is the one who has the same desires as everyone but who has learned to remain free and is preparing—gladly and seriously—to live a real adventure. That person prefers to give up short-lived, easy tricks in order to be fully available when the day comes that someone wants to embark on an adventure with him or her. How many young people find themselves trying to act cool in the evening, convinced that this is how they will pass as "normal"? They can be so afraid of appearing stuck or corny. How many try to list their conquests to reassure themselves or to feel sure in the eyes of others? They then justify their actions by saying that it is nothing, or just a game without any major consequences, and that both parties are fully aware of what they are doing. They even try to accentuate the playful side of things by having contests or by challenging each other during the evening. They boast about themselves without a care about their reputation. But ultimately, you will one day approach the girl or boy you love in the same way. It is, therefore, not a harmless act. Besides, who would enjoy seeing their beloved "nab" another? Even just for fun? And let's be honest. At sixteen, it is all done in the spirit of lightness and fun. Except that the same thing happens at eighteen years of age; they find themselves just as lightly going up to the bedroom. As they are half drunk, it quickly escalates and it goes pretty far. Too far. In such a smutty way.

How sad it is when I hear young people confide in me that their "first time" was after an evening of having too much to drink—with a friend, or a stranger, or even with the person they loved and with whom they were getting serious. But under the influence of a few drinks, all good intentions vanished. They ended up doing something not so skillfully. Without really respecting each other. Without really choosing to do it. And the next day, they regret having gone too fast. It is not really what they had imagined.

Not so fast! How can we believe that a long-lasting adventure can take hold in just a few days? Yet is this not the usual picture? They meet at a party, they may have already kissed. They exchange phone numbers, they meet the next day for coffee, they send text messages—increasingly more personal—throughout the following week. The next weekend, they are in love, convinced that there is something meaningful. They start going out together, just "to see."

Because it is better than being alone. Because they are afraid to miss their chance. Because others have encouraged them. Sure, they talked about it with their friends on the second day of their meeting. And now they are a charming new couple with an official announcement and photos on Facebook. Please do not call it love! It is a caricature of love. One cannot offer oneself so fast. One cannot give of oneself so fast. One cannot promote oneself so fast.

Love needs time. Love needs discretion. Love needs patience. Nothing should interfere with a budding romance between two serious young people. They do not need the external influences that might spoil what they are trying to slowly build. The first tender gestures are not meant to be displayed in public. There is no need to exhibit these tender moments after school, kissing in front of everyone. What is it that you need to demonstrate? How could you bear people saying that you have been "exploited" if you truly do not have the ambition to live through one more "love affair."

I believe in love at first sight. Of course! One can fall completely head over heels in love in a single encounter. But nothing keeps you, especially when you are young, from taking the time to get to know each other. Invite him, take her out with your group of friends or among others. Meet up with others. Go on a holiday, to the WYD (!), out for the weekend, on a pilgrimage, or on an expedition with several others. Go be of service together, side by side, helping the young and the poor. There is nothing better to really get to know someone. You reveal yourself best in a group of people, in community, and over the long haul. Have projects to complete and to experience together. Create some memories, strong and memorable experiences that you will share in common.

Even if your heart is protected, give your intelligence some space. It also needs to work. Do you share the essentials needed to build a common history? Do you share fundamental beliefs about love and how you each prepare for it? You can be in love with someone very different from you, someone with opposite persuasions. But dating someone without thinking that you might one day truly commit yourselves, why do it? I am not saying that you must be absolutely certain from day one that this will be your partner for life. But you must start from this perspective: "If I am picking up early signs that it will not be possible to start a family together, then why be a couple? To pass the time? To gather some experience? For fun? This did not prepare me at all for the future. I am wasting my time, and I especially risk giving my partner the hope of something that I am not able to give them. And a romance with no tomorrow and no future can hurt and leave marks."

This is essential: when you decide to date someone, it is primarily after you have made a personal discernment and within the context of a mutual discernment to see if you are made for each other, if you want to permanently engage. You have to feel it deep in your heart and be able to readily share it with the other. It is precisely because you have a potential commitment on the horizon that you can foster discernment by asking the right questions, by honestly sharing your truth and learning to know one another in light of this project.

Are you not just looking for a short-term emotional fix when you go out with someone without any sense of commitment? In all sincerity, this means that you are using the other person. Just like they are using you. But it is not in the spirit of giving. Some will say, "How can you expect that at sixteen or eighteen years old, one might be able to start questioning themselves about commitment or engagement?" I totally agree with you. This is proof that you must wait; now is simply not the time.

Not so fast also means to not be afraid to take a step back. Distance is essential for discernment. When you have your nose to the grindstone, you see nothing. When you take a step back, you can have better a perspective on the scenery and understand where you are going. This distance is valuable for those who are in love. When you love, you tend to see everything as you would like it to be. The illusion can be so easy. So can self-justification.

One way to take distance is to go talk with a priest or a nun you know and in whom you trust, to share what you are going through: your questions, your judgments, your joys and difficulties. This "big brother" or "big sister" is not emotionally attached to your story. They have the necessary perspective to help you face things directly and stay true to yourself.

It is out of the question that the priest will make a decision for you. But he will help you find good judgment. He may suggest some of the questions you can ask yourself. He will alert you about the risks you run. He will be able to encourage you on this journey of learning to love. I am always reassured when I see a boy or a girl capable of such openness. Despite the difficulties, they are at least not lying to themselves. Do not be afraid of the questions that the priest may ask. If your story is beautiful and if your heart is clear, you will not be afraid to let him question you. It is not good to lock everyone out in order to be sure you will not lose the one you love. It is better to learn to make a clear and solid decision. Your choice, but a real choice.

Taking some distance also means accepting that you will not see each other all the time right away. Blessed are those lovers who do not live in the same city. Blessed are those who go study abroad for six months! Why? Because these times of separation will allow each person to assess what attracts them to each other. What do you like about each other? What is lacking in your relationship? Do they miss you after all? The separation can allow you to naturally put the brakes on the sensitive nature of the relationship so you can enter more consciously into it. To find the right balance between the excitement of a moment and the lasting, deeply rooted feeling.

I beg of you, do not be afraid of this distance. And do not try to reduce it by filling the space with hundreds of text messages. There is nothing worse. It is an artificial way of keeping the other close to you, but it does some damage on the benefits of distance. You tend to reveal yourself a lot faster by text message, and it is not very natural. You would not be so revealing when you are in person with the other. People tend to also argue and misunderstand each other over the phone. How can you imagine resolving disputes or asking important questions by phone or text message? And yet I have stopped counting the number of people who claim their connection by text or break up on a phone call. This is distressing. To build and nurture the relationship, may I suggest to you a thousand times to write a letter. Not an email; a letter! They came to see you this weekend? Very good. When you escort them to the train station, and while on the platform, thank them for the time spent together. Then go home and take the time to meditate, write, and reread what you have experienced together, your exchanges and conversations. Think about what you want to remove, what you will keep. Do not immediately send ten text messages. He is on the train; do not worry. Do not call him in the evening. Or even the next day. Hold back a little. Respect this time of freedom. You are not committed to each other yet. Do not worry about what she is doing, who she is seeing. Take the time to let what you experienced ripen. Then, if you really want to communicate, write him a really nice letter to share what you got out of your exchanges.

A letter is one hundred times more effective because you took the time to choose the words, to make sentences, and to think about what you want to write. You find the right tone and you devote yourself to it. When you receive a letter, you know the time that the other has spent writing it. You read and reread it quietly. You have time to respond. You are not reacting off the cuff or from instinct. A letter stays with you longer. You can refer back to it whenever you want. Letters and real, face-to-face conversations are the building blocks. It is not the same with text messages. Do not be prisoners of your relationship. Do not chain yourselves together with these text messages, the emails, and the endless calls. It is not about creating a dependency between you; it is about allowing yourself to have a choice. How many relationships end up being stifling for one or the other without being able to admit it?

Not too fast—this also means taking the time to discover your vocation. I am convinced that many dedicated vocations are lost because of these flirtations and other short adventures that are engaged in too soon and too fast. How can you faithfully and freely discern what God wants for you if your heart is already encumbered? Falling in love is not necessarily a sign that you are not called to be a priest or a nun! To experience the feeling of love is human and natural, whatever your vocation. But if the Lord calls you to devote yourself to him, you have to learn to control your feelings. You will have to give up the love of another for the purpose of a greater love, this time. You will give yourself totally to God and to all. This is another reason to learn to hold yourself back, in order to give better to yourself. It will be hard to give up the love of a girl or a boy if you have become accustomed to these easy hugs or these flings.

Not Too Close!

Make no mistake. This in no way means that you need to feel any discomfort in relation to the body. Neither yours nor that of the other. The Christian religion grants a certain importance to the body—we believe that God made flesh!—and teaches respect for the body as a "temple of the Holy Spirit."

One can never say it enough: sexuality, the union of body, the game of love, sexual pleasure and desire—this is all good because God wanted it and created it. This is really beautiful and significant! Any speech that despises the body, that finds sexuality "dirty" or views it as an act of sin, is in no way Christian. It would soon prove how unbalanced a perspective it is.

Simply stated, everything must be in its right place. The body is there to serve the heart and the intelligence. It is not there to rule but to serve. In fact, in the words of John Paul II, it is necessary that "the gestures of the body be the language of the heart."[2] What the heart has

chosen is the body responsibility to demonstrate it. Thus the body does not anticipate the
heart's choices; instead, it reveals them. And if
there is a lag between the body and the heart—
when the body is given without the heart's con-
sent—then there is injury, a rupture.

Too many young people are left internally
"broken" or "torn" because the body no longer follows the impulses of the heart. It made
a habit of giving itself without engaging the
heart at the same time. Often one can come to
despise one's body. Actions no longer have any
value, as if we were no longer ourselves in our
bodies. We give our bodies without really giving of ourselves. "Not too close" means do not
let your bodies get any closer if your hearts are
not ready to open up and commit.

Not too close also means do not be afraid of
acts of love. Do not be afraid of acts of tenderness. Do not be afraid to learn to perform such
acts, while gradually adjusting to the situation,
but be aware that no gesture is insignificant.
Our actions can be deeply affecting. Our bodies have a memory. There is no option to tread
lightly in this area. Here, more than ever, we
must go with care, respect, and sensitivity.

One day at the end of a conference in Paris, a young woman came to me. She explained that, for a year, she went out with a boy. "In fact, you know him well," she told me. "After a year, he wanted to end our relationship. Since then, he has moved on. As for me, I've been unable to do anything for the last year." What happened? I can attest that this young man is a good guy. Really. I just think they were not careful enough. They did not take it to the end, but they were driven by their actions and words. And they were not necessarily able to discern if the other person felt the same way about actions within the relationship. I think she felt more involved by their acts of tenderness than he did. In the end, it felt to her as if he had used her, as if he did not have the same sense of reality that she had. She felt hurt. For her, if he said what he had to say, and if he offered a particular gesture of tenderness, that meant he was ready and he had chosen her. He very sincerely did not give the same meaning to his gestures. He did not feel as committed as she felt. How could she accuse him of lying to her? He always felt he had been sincere, and that was the case. One can "sincerely" err.

So should you keep from engaging in these acts? Of course not! There is such beautiful learning in allowing the tenderness to unfold gradually. But this must be done by dialoguing, taking time to talk about and reflect on each person's intentions. Take time to explain to each other how you react to what he or she does and says. Boys and girls do not react the same way to the amorous solicitations of another. You do not have the same attitude toward the body; that is a given! You must learn to know, to understand how the other person operates. What may seem trivial to one person is likely different for the other. Your desires are not the same; neither is your sensibility. That is why you have to prove you are able to attend to the other person's needs. You need to offer infinite respect and great delicacy to your desire for closeness.

Not too close also means finding the true meaning of innocence. Unfortunately, innocence has become a sign of stuckness or frustration, while it is really a sign of courage and true freedom. With innocence, you do not repress your desires, but you learn to work with them in order to master them. The stakes are high:

it's about letting the heart and intelligence govern instead of the desires and impulses.

This purity of heart is never achieved once and for all; it is the fruit of a long labor. You do not learn to be inwardly free and self-controlled in a few months. The way through is hard and demanding; we are all weaklings when it comes to this. But it is also a beautiful inner struggle. A boy or a girl who fights to keep this clarity of heart and mind will one day be able to offer the fruit of this struggle to their loved one. This is the driving force of the fight, the main reason to not get discouraged: we fight for the one we love! We do this in order to have clear intentions toward them, in order to never damage them with any lingering selfishness or gaps in clarity.

Personal purity is a tough battle; it can be this way especially for boys and especially at the age of one's formation. At this age, it is often more difficult to control our impulses and our physical desires. For some, it is a daily struggle. It can be exhausting—and discouraging. Masturbation and pornography can become addictive. Some will hide these things behind a facade of politeness, while others are conversely unashamed, as if nothing was seriously wrong with them. But deep inside, there is a desire for freedom in this area: to not fall over oneself so stupidly, to not be angry, to not feel disgusted or ashamed of finding pleasure in these degrading images. "This is not what I want . . . but it's stronger than me!" How many times have I heard someone express this so painfully!

Let's be clear: it's essential to understand that people do fail. The battle is often very challenging, but it exists for everyone, one way or another. Would anyone dare say otherwise? Would anyone dare claim that they are strong and confident in this area? Would anyone dare be the first to cast a stone? The key is perseverance, your desire to remain clear, to never be discouraged. To a group of young Germans, Pope Benedict XVI said, "At the end of your life, the Lord will not count the number of times you have fallen; He will count the number of times you have picked yourself back up."[3] The key is to recognize that you are on the way, to get up undeterred, and to gradually learn to choose what is truly joyful by turning away from easy, ephemeral, and inevitably disappointing pleasures.

For the one you love, you cannot offer a flawless CV . . . would that you protect your humility! You will tell them of the times you picked yourself up, one time after another, as evidence that, as you kept them in mind, you were never discouraged, you never gave up. Remember, what you are experiencing today is preparing the husband or the wife you will be tomorrow. Let me tell you about the man whose joy is made palpable by his efforts and his victories as he shares them with his fiancée, for her, and thanks to her! Indeed, he is a happy and proud man who is able to say to his bride, "You know, it's hard for us boys, but to deserve you, to be able to love you, I gradually learned to control myself. I picked myself up, I never gave up, I always held hope." Blessed are those boys who have enough simplicity not to justify their weaknesses or to recklessly laugh about them but to face them courageously without ever losing their zest for life, to overcome them step by step while allowing themselves to get help when necessary.

Blessed are the youth who seek support from friends in their fight for innocence! Here again, social pressure may affect the most sensitive of us. It may be cool, sometimes, to laugh about or to minimize things. "After all, we're still young! It sounds fun!" Once again, one gets caught in the fear of appearing inflexible, without even thinking about the risk of becoming trapped in degrading habits. Be careful. It is not about dramatizing or relativizing everything either. It is about wanting and choosing one's friendships so they take you to greater heights, including in this area. You need friends, not accomplices.

Blessed are the young people who learn to love each other by sharing this desire for clarity. Not that they are obsessed with the sins they should not be committing. But they feel a precious desire to want to help one another find that joyful and positive innocence that facilitates discernment. Here lies the real proof of their sensitivity: Rather than simply being driven by their own desires—which can sometimes be a little dictatorial—they prefer to listen to another's needs in order to better respect them. And to encourage each other. To pull one another up and to allow the other to give the best they have to offer.

On the contrary, when a couple is in a race to the bottom by imitating the habits of the

least-demanding party, they should seriously
be wondering what they are doing. Love makes
people grow. It should not diminish people or
make them give up. And if either is not as ful-
filled or does not have the same requirements as
the other, they will always gain more by learning from the one who has the most demanding
and greater goal. What a joy to discover in the
other this new way of loving for real. Two people will progress better by setting a high goal—
by choosing the highest peak to climb. Isn't it
the greatest proof that we love another person
by helping them to grow, by allowing them to
demonstrate the best they can be?

This is not to say there must be "zero mistakes" here as well. Often we grow step by step,
and this rarely happens without missteps. But
what matters is that we want to persevere. The
innocence will then often be synonymous with
humility—and even humor!

Blessed, indeed, are those who know they
are not stronger than any other person, who
know themselves and choose to simply follow
the basic rules of the game together to help
each other live with innocence! Blessed are
those who humorously recognize that they are

not naturally champions at chastity and who therefore exercise caution in order to not get into complicated situations. Blessed are those who engage in the rules of the game not as a burdensome yoke, but as an open path toward preparing for the day when they are ready to fully offer themselves.

Not too close—this is a good basic rule, not to keep you from offering yourself but to better help you wait for the day when the gift of yourself will be a truth to behold. Not too close—it reminds me of this conversation:

"Father, I'm really happy; she's coming to see me this weekend. She's coming up to Paris; from Lyon, that's pretty fast. We will have time to share."

"Great! So tell me, did you find a hotel room that's not too expensive?"

"Uh . . . no. In Paris it costs too much. I'm studying. I have very little to spend."

"She'll stay with one of your friends then?"

"Uh . . . that's not really what we planned. In fact, she's planning on staying with me."

"Oh, that's cool. You have a spare room?"

"Nope. I just have a dorm room, you know."

"So you're going to sleep in the living room?"

"Oh no! It's really only a dorm room. The size of a bed. The living room is my room. So is my shower and my kitchen. It's 110 square feet—that's what, the size of a bed."

"Ah. And you plan to sleep on the floor?"

"Uh, honestly, we didn't really plan too much. But . . . but my Father, what do you imagine? Nothing will happen, I promise you!"

"You're kidding me! You're in love with her, she's beautiful and crazy in love with you. You'll spend two nights in a single bed too small for you, and you want to make me believe that you'll settle for playing a board game? You think I'm a 'c,' or are you a 'c'?"[3]

Some people's naiveté is amazing. But is this really naive? I think that at this stage, it is a little more about guilt. An old priest spoke of the "sin of the doormat." To the young man who came to confess of having "slipped" with his girlfriend, he said, "Your real sin is not to have had sex with her. It was to have brought her home with you at that hour. In other words, for having crossed the doormat! That's the moment when, in your head, you flip a switch. You know how it all might end, and you still take the risk."

Just do not sleep together. Period. Not just because the situation is a bit risky but also because it is not well-adjusted. The other person's room, their bed, belongs to their privacy. One does not enter another person's privacy with so little intention. We must wait for these words to be spoken on the day of the wedding: "I will receive you and I will give myself to you." We must wait to be received. This is an important aspect of relationship. When we love each other, it is not just about "avoiding sin." It is also about seeking what is the fairest, the best—what is actually well-adjusted. This is also more affirmative. It is good to take the steps to stay real, to enlighten one's conscience, to consult with a priest, to read, and to pray. Your conscience will then alert you. You will feel great if what you do is well-adjusted, if your motives are clear, if you have dedicated your life to the path or if you want to commit yourself to it. We spend so little time developing our conscience, yet it is such a valuable compass—as long as we listen to it.

Not too close—I would like to express my admiration for the young couples, and even the betrothed, who dedicate themselves to this

gift of chastity. I admire those who choose to
or want to learn to live in joyous, affirmative,
and loving chastity. They offer themselves to
the other as a precious gift, in order to be better prepared to love. I admire the young people
who have already had sex but who, after taking
a break, having a long heart-to-heart talk or
a good confession with a priest, are inspired
to rediscover the beauty of chastity. I admire
the young people who trust the Church to be
there for them. I give thanks for the joy they
share with me. "Father, we didn't think we
would be able . . . it's hard sometimes . . . but
we already see the results! We're rediscover-
ing each other. We pay more attention to each
other. We achieve a certain depth."

Their efforts, their gains, their perseverance
in trying to do their best—all that touches the
heart of God very deeply. This is a far cry from
any heavy moralism. Instead, it is a very generous proposition. Since your relationship can
be the most beautiful thing you have, will you
agree to take the steps toward building it? Do
you agree to do your best and to accept the
"instructions" that the wise Church offers you?
Do you agree to then offer this to the one you

love? We are a far cry from frustration. We are in the realm of dedication.

This makes me rethink, with a smile, of this young engaged couple, twenty-three and twenty-four years old: still very young. They wanted to live in chastity, but like for most of their peers, it was challenging. Especially for him. But they were effortful. They did their best. One day, they told me that it was really hard when they saw each other late at night in their bedroom. I told them, "But of course it's challenging! When you get together to talk late into the night, sitting on one another's bed in a dorm room that is barely bigger than the size of the bed, it's not surprising that you have other ideas quickly come to mind. At this point, you need to be a hero to say no."

It just so happens that there was a kebab restaurant close by, one of those restaurants that stays open all night. I told them, "If you really need to see each other late into the night, go to the kebab restaurant to talk. The smell of fries and sandwiches will curb all your zeal." She was thrilled with the idea, especially since she loved to talk. He, on the other hand, was a little upset with me.

During the latter part of their engagement, I often received text messages from her at one in the morning: "Thank you, Father. Because of you, we're having another kebab!" On their wedding day, amid the acknowledgments on the last page of the Mass booklet, there was a reference that I believe few people understood: "Thanks to Father Grosjean for his help, his tips, and the many kebabs we ate because of him." They didn't say it maliciously. As for me, I laughed and gave thanks for their good humor.

I cannot help believing that God was the first to be amused with lingering around the kebabs; He was probably touched by their humility and their desire to do well. They knew they were weak, and they had the humility to recognize and to take simple steps toward their ideal. Never has a kebab been such a sign of one's desire for love.

Not too close—this means, finally, do not play with certain edges. Sometimes there is a certain hypocrisy in not "taking it to the limit," that is, not giving themselves totally to the other in a full sexual relationship but still allowing all that precedes it—as if the Church's message was simply to impose a red line that should not be crossed. We are talking primarily about a state of mind. I think that even the preliminary explorations, since that is what we are addressing, may even be more hurtful. Of course, you did not take it "to the limit." But what did you do? You played with the other person's body; you used it for your pleasure. This is not self-sacrifice; it is using the other person to your advantage. In such actions there is something unfulfilling, an in-between, something unsatisfactory and affectively missing. It is basically nothing more than masturbation with two people. This is what hurts. "How can someone who loves me ask this of me? How can someone who loves me do this?" You are made for the gift of self; you are a complete gift—when you're ready. You are not made to give half of yourself, to "grab" each other, to touch each other. All this is rather fundamental. And beyond the pleasure of a moment, you will understand that there is ultimately little satisfaction to be had.

If God's mercy can forgive and repair many mistakes, at least try to not get used to this kind of more or less appropriate "slippage." Often the first time you do it, you went "too far" or "far enough" without really meaning to. You had a few drinks, you were in love, you were excited by the other person, you got carried away. I give thanks for those who consequently become aware of what they have done and use this error to immediately start on a solid foundation. They immediately go to confession, they lay their cards out on the table, and then they take steps to avoid failing again. They will have learned that they are weak and that even the best can fail. They become more attentive and more humble. But those who minimize the situation, who don't care, who continue having fun or boasting about their exploits—they take the risk to repeat their behavior and to become quickly addicted to these emotionally deprived relationships and these actions that leave very little room for love. Without realizing it, they only imitate what they have seen in porn flicks. They want to be "liberated," and they reassure themselves by saying that this is not going too far, but the concept of what's "too far" is a moving target.

I beg of you, do not let yourself be mired in these traps. The mucky, sad souls of so many young people who are deeply despondent in light of their weakness, who are damaged and soiled by their repeated sins, is a phenomenon that leaves no priest indifferent. Let us get you out of there. Let us help you free yourself. Let us give you the taste of what is real! Let us give you back the clarity of a child of God who is made to love and be loved. Not made for "nabbing," "shagging," or "sleeping with," but rather made for "love" and for "giving" of oneself—for real.

Quality
Friendships

This need for realness is difficult to live with and to grow if we remain isolated. This is another key issue of your foundational years: to build strong friendships that help you stay healthy and that bring the best out of you. How lucky you are to have a group of friends with whom you can feel encouraged and free to share how you want to create beauty in your life. This luck must be earned. Have courage to choose your friends and make time to cultivate real friendships. The quality of these friendships—boys and girls—is a wonderful asset for the person who truly wants to learn to love.

I would like to tell you what I expect of both girls and boys. You have, indeed, each a valuable role for each other.

For Girls!

Ladies! You probably already know the boys' drama. Their number-one problem is that they are weak. Boys are often softies. Laziness is *the* great sin for boys. I say it humbly—but it's so true. We are very indecisive: we are first to start many amazing projects, to cultivate great desires, to want to travel the world, offer our lives as heroes, create our businesses, build an empire, and . . . we're unable to make our bed, wax our shoes, tidy our room, sit down at our desk. This requires an almost superhuman effort.

The preferred verb tense of boys is the conditional: "It should have . . ." "It would be nice if . . ." "I would like to . . ." In short, we have a real problem with our will. Why tell you this? Because you have to realize, dear young women, the impact you have on our human will.

Guy de Larigaudie—one of the first Scout leaders who wrote *Étoile au grand large*,[1] a small book that can be read and reread—offers a fun test that you can try out next summer. Imagine a pool with some boys around it. There is a very high diving board. None of them will go up there to dive, either because they are too lazy or because they are scared. Bring in two or three young girls who are very friendly, dressed in "summer" attire, who come to rest at the edge of the pool. The boys' reaction will be immediate. They will rush to the diving board, jostling to be the first to jump, making a beautiful swan dive. It works every time. And it's great! The simple gaze of a girl helps a boy overcome his fear or laziness. Where once these gentlemen were either too fearful or too lazy ten minutes before, they now excel and try to merit a glance from one of these girls. Can you see the positive impact of a female presence on a group of boys?

Seriously, I think the attitude of a group of friends depends largely on the attitude of these girls. I do not mean to say that they are solely responsible if this group of friends goes off on a tangent or devolves into neglectfulness. It would be too easy to blame another group for the foolishness committed by one group! But I give thanks to heaven when, among a group of male and female friends, I see young, beautiful, cheerful, and lively girls who are also discriminating, liberated, and able to say no; clear and bright girls who invite us to give the best of what we have.

I often hear boys tell me, "You know, Father, I met a great girl this evening. Immediately upon being with her, I felt I wanted to be a gentleman." What a blessing for a boy to come across girls who uplift him and keep him from floundering or from getting bogged down in his weakness or laziness; girls who inspire him to find the strength and the will to get back up, to progress, and to offer the best of himself.

I also want to add something for you girls. Boys face a really tough fight, especially at the age when they are building a foundation: it is the struggle of personal purity. I have already talked about it. It is often more difficult for a boy to learn self-control and to acquire inner freedom. Their impulses are strong; they are often overwhelmed by physical desire. Pornography and masturbation are frequent temptations. For some, even among the best, these behaviors become addictions because it is so difficult to learn to say no to these immediate pleasures, which are easily accessible but ephemeral.

In this fight, which is often a secret battle, the boy struggles against sadness and discouragement, leaving scars of his failures and his relapses deep inside the heart. He feels especially frustrated because his state of being does not correspond to what he knows he can achieve. He sometimes disgusts himself and loses confidence. Many dare not entrust the details of this fight in confession and end up carrying too heavy a burden without seeking any kind of help. This might be the hardest thing to bear.

But in this fight that you often ignore or whose violence you do not perceive, you, ladies, have a valuable role: I'm not talking about confessing on behalf of your male friends or having a morbid curiosity toward their problems. Instead, I'm suggesting you offer him your bright friendship, a friendship of clarity and trust. Often, to earn that trust, a boy will find the courage to not stay stuck. To deserve your friendship, he will find the strength to not stay discouraged and to pick himself back up. By being in your presence, he can sense this clarity in you and he will develop a desire for it in himself. Just like a group of boys will readjust themselves in their conversation when a girl joins them, they will also learn—from being in your presence— the tremendous respect that is required when approaching you. This requires that they not let themselves get into messy situations or wallow in deceitful pleasures. I am always moved when a boy tells me about the girl he loves, or about such and such a great friend, and then he tells me how he would be messing things up if he got bogged down in pornography or impurity.

Warning: this is not about requiring boys to be perfect. We are all struggling, especially in this area. And even if we know that not everyone falls, or that not everyone falls as much as the other, everyone knows how fragile they are and that they need to remain vigilant. But it is about encouraging these boys by your mere presence. It is your mission to be the clarity of their lives as men. Encourage them by showing them how sensitive you are to their efforts, how much you love to feel their honesty and clarity in turn. How especially what touches your heart will not be your fiancé's "perfection" but his ability to never be discouraged as he picks himself up from each fall. The most courageous act for our boys is not to never fall but to persevere. You are, often unwittingly, the reason for this perseverance: be conscious of it.

Boys!

Gentlemen, you know the girls' "drama"? Their biggest problem is that they are complicated. Infinitely complicated. The heart of a young girl is complicated; you cannot imagine. Why? Because in the heart of every girl, there is a fear—conscious or not—that she will not be chosen, loved, considered, recognized for who she is. And so there is also the need, conscious or not, to be constantly reassured by seeking this attention, this interest, from the boys. Just to be reassured and to be appeased. Consider these two examples.

I happened to go on vacation with a group of high school juniors[2]—thirteen boys and girls. They were friendly young people who had invited me to come with them for a few relaxing days in the vacation home of one of them. It was an opportunity to have good conversations while relaxing a bit. (I also want to encourage you to not hesitate to ask your priest to go on vacation with your group of friends.) I am always amused to see the difference in the size of bags people take. A boy might be content with merely his school bag for a week's outing, whereas his female friends arrive with two suitcases the size of a table! They have three outfits for each day.

So one day the boys and I were in the living room, talking. Then one of the girls, a lovely young woman, comes down the stairs in her midafternoon outfit, which certainly was made to showcase her beauty and the assets that the Creator had generously given her. She shows up in the living room, all radiant. Without realizing it, the boys completely stopped listening to me and their gaze followed the trajectory of their female friend. She just sits on the sofa between two guys—I was surprised to find there was room—and she ends her trajectory by gently placing her hand on the knee of one of the boys. Looking cute, all smiles, she was reassured: she had accomplished what she needed. For her, it was enough. The boys, unfortunately, were all twisted up inside.

This story is not completely trivial. How many young girls, just for the sake of reassurance, light a fire in a boy that they then fail to master? How many girls have gone further than they wanted to, simply because they wanted some attention, tenderness, and support but then realized the boy wanted even more?

Here is another concrete example: this is a fun test you can try once you have finished reading this book. You hear that math class is cancelled tomorrow afternoon because your teacher is sick. You cross paths with one of your female friends—she is simply a friend—in the hallway, and you ask her out for coffee the next day, since you are both getting out of class earlier. She agrees and thanks you. You leave her and go to your rugby training. What will she do a few seconds after you leave, not long after you have turned your back on her? She takes her cell phone and calls her best friend.

"Hello, you know what? Peter asked me out for coffee!"

"Really? But why ?"

"Well . . . I don't know. Do you think it could be an invitation or a kind of response to what I might have said without saying much on Friday evening?"

"I don't know. But if you want, I know his cousin. I met him at *Paray-le-Monial*[3] this summer. I can ask him on Facebook if he knows something, or perhaps he can give me some information."

And here, as the brave boy is busy playing rugby and having already forgotten about the next day's coffee date, the girl, in turn, spends the next twenty-four hours fantasizing about the meaning of the coffee date, engaging the whole world in helping her understand the hidden purpose of this invitation—there has to be a purpose, from her perspective—and how to prepare for this important date.

What are the greatest lessons we can draw from this?

First, gentlemen, take time to reassure your friends. Tell them often and regularly that you love them as they are: uncomplicated and natural. Tell them that they can stop worrying. Reassure them by showing them that you pay attention to each of them, for who they are, for their special gifts, and that they don't need to constantly be looking for reassurance, sometimes even somewhat artificially.

Beyond that, never play with the feelings of another. And this is true both for boys and for girls. You saw how a simple coffee date can stir up a lot of hope for the one you are inviting. So imagine what might happen with a hasty text message, a quickly given kiss, an "I love you" offered a little too early, a gesture of tenderness given too lightly, a secret revealed too quickly, and even more seriously, her body offered too fast and too soon. All of these things can make someone hope for something you are not willing to promise, you are not able to offer. Here is how you can really hurt each other. Do not give up a coffee date. But be aware that your actions and your words are binding and influential.

And gentlemen, also pay attention to one thing: pornography. If there is indeed a misdeed that damages your reputation with the girls, it is this one. I know that at age fourteen or fifteen, it makes boys laugh, especially with their classmates with whom they like to appear mature by showing off what they know. It is cool to not seem "stuck," to have seen everything and watched everything. What infinite sadness to see these young people who are already aged by sin and discover the acts of love through a dirty and brutish caricature.

As a priest who offers confession, I am deeply affected by how these images and movies wreak havoc on the hearts of many boys, well beyond their fifteen years of age. These are habits that you form, or rather they form you, and they may not let you go so easily. Fiancés and husbands come to confess and cry about these misdeeds that make them feel dirty as they look at the woman of their dreams.

Nobody is perfect. But here again, please understand that if you have a personal struggle with these issues, it is essential that you do not feel discouraged. Your fight is for the one you will love, to be able to look at her with a clear conscience, without any selfishness or polluted thoughts. You will give her a look that is respectful and loving, and not a possessive or demanding look.

It is a heroic struggle for many. Today, pornography is just a click away. The Internet has created a revolution in this area, and it has for the worse. When I was fifteen, there was no broadband. Of course, a few "friends" would pass around videotapes in the back of the classroom that guys would watch in the evening when their parents were out. They circulated porn magazines as well. But nothing was as easily accessible. I never had the guts to go to the newsstand to ask out loud for the magazine placed at the very top while three brave ladies were waiting to check out behind me. Besides, one of them probably knew my parents!

Today all you need is a computer or smartphone and access to the neighbor's Wi-Fi network to be able to see the worst. Otherwise the family computer can also be used, although it has an access code. (Often parents use their wedding anniversary as the code for parental controls. What a blessed and pathetic naiveté on behalf of our dear parents!) This ease of access increases the risk of addiction. Porn is like a drug. During a few minutes of viewing, the outside world no longer exists. One retreats into an imaginary world and gets immediate satisfaction, but this eventually gives way to a great void, a sadness, and a bitter taste. As soon as you take a step back, you realize that it is so miserable. It is so distant from what you really want to create. And yet relapses are so easy and the habit so easily formed. It is just like a drug: you must gradually seek more "trashy" stuff" in order to be satisfied. A vicious cycle is set in place. So many damaged hearts? So many veiled glances?

Yes, sometimes it is heroic to resist. And I deeply admire those who are willing to receive the help, the encouragement, the boost that they need. We are all at times vulnerable. Especially when we are forming ourselves. We must then find the humility to come confess our misdeeds and let ourselves be given a boost. Not only does God's forgiveness liberate us from the heaviness of guilt and release us from the sadness of sin, but it also restores, encourages, and strengthens us gradually.

We must find the humility to recognize we are weak and agree to take the steps that will help us stay the course. We can quickly learn about ourselves and identify the "scenario" that led us to the misdeeds. It is then better to flee dangerous situations rather than face the ongoing temptations. I do not recommend staying up late—too late—in front of the screen, or hanging out aimlessly surfing the Internet, or connecting "for no reason," just because you are bored. I do recommend that each person decide whatever small concrete steps they can take, adapted to their capability, so they do not end up in difficult situations.

One day, I suggested to a student that he place a small image of the Virgin Mary next to his screen. In this way, it would be difficult to visit a porn site with Our Lady's eyes staring at him. Three weeks later he came back to me, saying, "Well, Father, your idea of the small image of the Virgin Mary was a good one. But in my case, I would need a large poster!"

Well, OK . . . we all need concrete steps of some kind. It is up to each person to figure out what can help. In any case, you can be sure of one thing: once you are engaged to be married, you will understand that it was worth it not to get discouraged. You will be happy to provide the one you love with these successive recoveries and to show that your perseverance has borne fruit. Never give up!

This is what I want for you boys and girls. This is why I give thanks to heaven when you take the time to build strong groups of friends. Within them you will find there is no race toward seduction. Instead, there is an open, clear, and supportive environment in which boys and girls can learn to embody this purity of heart. May it be especially joyful and positive. It is not about focusing constantly on sin or, even worse, being suspicious of everything. It is mostly about helping each other do well, about finding in our friendships the joy of altruism and an anchoring in the true joys of life. We are then vaccinated against false pleasures, and we prepare ourselves for love. At age fifteen to twenty, this is the time of building great friendships that are free and clear and that make you grow and build your character.

A Comment on Homosexuality

It would be useful to write an entire book to explain with greater precision and clarity the message of the Church on this subject. Why talk about it here? Because the quality of friendships that we just talked about plays a part in this. And, like with many things, God is not ignorant on the matter. Let's explore this.

The homosexual tendency that some carry in them, whether exclusive or not, has never been chosen. It is about a kind of personal injury, like we all carry—sometimes for a very long time—on some level without ever knowing where it comes from. Our relationships within our families, the roles of our father and mother, how we received our education—these all mark us in unique and complex ways. Many also carry the wound of a sexual assault or unhappy experiences that marked their discovery of sexuality.

This here is not the proper place to study all this in detail. What is certain is that you are not responsible for this tendency in yourself. You are responsible for how you will live with it, because you have the freedom to choose or you can learn that freedom. It is also for this reason that the Church never condemns people's homosexuality; it will never confine a person to their sexual orientation or by what they will sometimes do and act upon.

When I meet young people who discover their homosexuality, I first tell them this: "You are primarily a person, infinitely richer and more complex than a label that society would like to stick on you. Do not close yourself off, and do not let yourself be closed off as well. Never forget that God loves you as you are, for who you are. Some people have such difficulty understanding or accepting their vulnerability. Knowing that you are loved is what's most essential."

Because the Church wants what's best for you, it cannot mislead you. Relative to the distinction I made earlier in this book, the Church recognizes that there may exist really sincere homosexual relationships. But there will never be that fullness of truth that man's heart needs, an essential characteristic will always be missing: the radical otherness of man and woman, this complementarity of sexual identities for which our bodies and our hearts are made. This otherness is the only way to bring forth life.

That is why the Church believes that engaging in same-sex relationships, even sincerely, will never be a path that we support. Because we believe it will never be fulfilling. The Church prefers to tell the truth, even if it is painful, by offering you another way: that is, the way of chastity in abstinence. It is not about denying who you are, pretending or doing as if, but about gradually accommodating the reality of the Cross and choosing to courageously honor it and allow yourself to be helped.[4]

Here I would like to say how much I admire these young people that I know who live this reality that is both painful and luminous. No one doubts their stations of the cross. They had to mourn a married life just like others. And they looked for other ways to give of themselves, other fertile grounds, especially in the service of others and of little ones. This has never been easy. The path of chastity is challenging, and inner storms are not uncommon. The social climate does not help. One might feel as if walking on a ridge line; holding that burden can be a very lonely experience.

If you are in this situation, you reading this book, I beg of you: Let yourself be encouraged. Go see a benevolent priest. With his father's heart, he will accompany you, lift you up when necessary, and help you give real meaning to the sacrifices that you are called to make. He will help you find your way so you can give of yourself in another way. Yes, it sometimes looks like the way of the Cross. But it is also a way of life. Since the very first Easter, Jesus has assured us that our crosses will not have the last word at the end of our lives.

Other young people, for other reasons beyond their control, will need to mourn the possibility of marriage, family life, and the joys of married life. Many of them stay single for so many reasons. Yet they also feel within them the call for true love. Let us not underestimate the mourning that needs to happen. This is where we must remember the importance of friendships and the place of God.

Open, generous, and clear friendships are most valuable in supporting those who have to face these kinds of trials. The group of friends should not be intrusive. You should learn to help each other with your mutual challenges. Do not be selfish, especially when you learn to find your own way. It is essential that young couples or families continue to offer this delicate attention to those who are living alone, without closing them off or minimizing them into a particular state of being.

How I wish we could pay more attention to what we often say lightly or recklessly about a particular problem, and especially about homosexuality, without even thinking that one of our loved ones is being affected. The priest, who carries so many confidences, knows what everyone is feeling behind the facade. Let us have an infinite amount of attention toward other people. There are words, expressions, and jokes that hurt. As we are constantly reminded by Pope Francis, let us remember above all that God's unconditional love for each and everyone is primordial, before any judgment on or consideration of one another's life.

Finally, it seems to me that—for you who is living through these tests—God is the ultimate friend who can help make sense of what you think is a painful cross. Only He can fully understand you. He knows you; He understands. He knows how much you too would have preferred to be able to love completely, to start a family, and to open yourself to life. He knows what may have hurt you. He knows you are not responsible for this. He knows.

In his eyes, you are unique, you are as valuable as any other person. His complete attention rests on you with amazement, knowing that you are beyond anything that could have been damaged. More than ever, more than all the others, commit your life to him. He wants it to be beautiful. He wants to give it another kind of fertility, a ray of light that will surpass your expectations. Your faithfulness in following him, in holding on to him in the sacraments and in prayer, and your trust—all of this will bear fruit. Your talents, your personality, who you are—God will help you put these in service of a purpose greater than you, in service of your brothers and of this world. You will find out how. You can gradually get there. Perhaps not all at once, not forever, not all the time. But don't ever lose heart. Let yourself be loved and encouraged.

And What about God in All of This?

At this stage of the book, you could offer me the following remark: "It's amazing. You do not say much about God in your remarks." It is true that everything I say could be appreciated by a nonbeliever. Is not the wisdom of the Church also relevant to those with good intentions who seek to live authentically? However, God is never absent. He stands in the background of all my remarks; He is the source of this topic. But what could we say more explicitly about his role?

God teaches me two essential truths, two bits of good news, for me to rediscover. This also provides an opportunity for many young people who have distanced themselves from him to find their way back to the Church and to prayer. There is one area in which we can really feel our limitations and we need God; that is the area of love. We want to succeed in love, yet we so often come up against our frailties, weaknesses, mistakes, or selfishness. That is why we need to hear these two pieces of good news.

With God, Nothing Is Lost

I have said it many times, but I will repeat it because it is so essential. I would not want one of you to think, "It's beautiful, it's grand, but for me it's too late. I've already abused myself. I'm too damaged. It's over."

Since I became a priest, which was almost ten years ago at the time of writing this book, I am probably touched the most by this reality, and it is the greatest joy of my priestly ministry: I have seen what God's mercy was able to accomplish in the hearts of those who let themselves be loved. Do not be afraid to rediscover the path of confession. Do not be afraid to make true confessions. They provide a place for forgiveness, for reconciliation, but also for healing. How many of you need this inner healing as you journey on the path of love and as you struggle for purity in your heart? How many need to reconnect with the joy of a pure heart and an open heart to learn to love? How many need to be forgiven by God in order to be able to forgive themselves their various past mistakes?

At the heart of the sacrament of confession, you can finally let go of the facade and allow yourself to be real. You can drop your faults, weaknesses, cowardice, discouragement, doubts, and defeats. You can finally identify what it is that soiled or damaged you. You can entrust your wounds and sorrows. Precisely because you will not be judged, much less condemned. Because God does not label us according to our sins. Because we are created in God's image, the priest greets you with the heart of a father who loves you and helps you get back on your feet. Indeed, his regard for you will never change. It is with great admiration that I listen to the confessions of these young people who sometimes have heavy burdens to release. I feel remorseful with them for their sins and the resulting damages, the pain and suffering that these sins may have caused. But I admire their honesty: at least they are being real. And I rejoice with them in the forgiveness that will give them back their identities as beautiful children of God.

What a joy to show them that they have always been loved by God who did "not come for the healthy, but for the sick and the sinners!"[1]

Of course you will more easily change your habits at fifteen than at eighteen years old, and at eighteen than at twenty-five years old. Do not delay until later the conversions you need to experience. Whatever your age, nothing is ever lost. Nobody is beyond redemption in the eyes of God. And, basically, there is as much courage in one who is careful and has kept oneself for the sanctity of marriage as there is in one who has perhaps fallen heavily but has then invested all their strength into getting back up, repairing things, and learning to love.

The real fight is the fight against discouragement and against despair. Let us never forget: the Lord himself will never be discouraged of us. He is even capable of finding a mysterious but true fecundity out of our trials and errors. Our efforts to gather ourselves will bear fruit. Our battles are not futile. That is why we must never lose confidence in ourselves and in God. He himself trusts us and continues to see in us what is great and beautiful—our desire for truth and goodness.

God Empowers Us

The second good news is that God empowers us toward happiness. It would be quite cruel of him to give us the capacity to love, the thirst for love and for being loved, and then leave us on our own.

Let no one say, "It's beautiful, but it's too hard for me." God wants to help you get ready for, and to one day realize, the joy of this great love. God will do nothing without you. He will not impose on you. But if you allow him to help you, He will.

This is the particular challenge of prayer and of the Eucharist.

In prayer we make ourselves available to the Lord so that He can act through us. Even if we do not feel anything, even if we see nothing, we prefer to believe that every single minute we offer to the Lord will be fecund. The Lord works on our hearts in silence; He prepares us and works on us to manifest his masterpiece in us. We will discover little by little what seemed at first impossible.

Take time to pray! Even one or two minutes per day. But do it every day. What makes our prayer beautiful is its loyalty. In the end, the content doesn't matter as much. Sometimes you will have trouble concentrating, or you will feel as if you are talking in a vacuum or have nothing to say. It does not matter. For God, it is simply our presence that matters—the time that we offer ourselves to him. He is working in the background. You will notice the fruits of your prayers in the long run. I prefer knowing of a young person who prays three minutes but every day versus another who prays half an hour when they feel like it. Like with any love, loyalty comes first—a freely given loyalty, beyond desire or lack of desire.

It is the same for Mass. We do not go to Mass because we "crave it." There certainly are days when we do not feel like going. Our loyalty should not depend on our moods or desires. Otherwise our spiritual life would go up and down like a seesaw. And then there is no stability.

Because Jesus wants to give of himself to us and love is at the heart of the Mass. Because love is at the heart of the Mass. And there is no greater injury than love that is given and not received. If we are not there, He really misses us. Again, you really need to establish yourself in a mature faith that is loyal and openly received.

In addition, there is no better school of love than Mass! Do you want to learn to love? Go to church! You will see what it means to love. You will hear Jesus tell you again, "This is my Body given for you" (Luke 22:19 NIV). Do you know any words of love that are stronger than the consecration? "This is my Body given for you," "This is my Blood, shed for you."[2] There are no words with a more relational sense than these. There is no better proof of love than these words. This is at the heart of the Mass. Jesus shows us how far true love can go: all the way to the complete gift of self, of one's life, of one's heart. When we give ourselves freely and mysteriously, we are deeply touched. This love is ultimate because Jesus gives himself to us through communion. We are one with him. And Jesus has come to love us. He has come to teach us to love, to show us how to love just as He loves.

Go to church! Who cares about the quality of the sermon, the songs, your neighbors' looks, the length of the announcements, or the church's architecture. All the better if it all looks perfect and leads us to pray. But it is only the shell of a mystery in which we have to enter: Jesus awaits us. We are so precious to him that He wants our presence. As He cried out on the Cross in his last breath, He "thirsts" to love us and make us capable of loving in return.

Regarding prayer, Mass, confession: Let's stop asking ourselves if we "feel like it" or "don't feel like it," if we have time or do not have time, if we feel something or not. Let's recognize that Jesus is waiting for us rather than waste our time recognizing ourselves. Let's choose to be present, to be faithful, and to be freely received, so that Jesus can act accordingly and so that his love can help us to love.

The only way to show someone that they are important to us is to spend time with them. When you love a girl or a boy, you know how to find the time to tell them and to show them. Your rhetoric is not enough; you need to be faithful to them, which is a sign of true love. It is important to be there when the other person is waiting for us or needs us. Your loyalty in responding to the Lord's call will be the foundation and the ongoing support for your loyalty to all your commitments, beyond your weaknesses.

When you do not pray, when you do not take communion, when you do not confess, you are left to your own devices. And very quickly you find out that they are limited. That is why when you are learning to love, there is space for the rediscovery of the spiritual life. A strong inner life will provide the backbone to sustain what you are building and experiencing. That is where you will find your joy.

With God, everything is possible. And this is also why we, as priests and consecrated ones, support you. We are called to be by your side as the representatives of the Lord Jesus's special attention. You are the reason for our consecration and our celibacy. We are called to love God with our whole being, entirely consecrated, "heart-body-soul" at his service; we are at your side, totally available to you. There will never be a reason for us to choose for you. But the priest is there to help you discern, to offer you some criteria that will allow you to make free choices. He is there to help you stay true to what you are going through. Because you know that in his company you will not be judged; you will be encouraged, supported, and heard.

Take advantage of the priests that the Lord puts on your path. Take the time to seek him out, this person in whom you trust. Know your vicar, your pastor, your high school or lower school or Scout unit chaplain. Overcome your resistance and dare to engage in real conversations with him about what you are experiencing. How many times have I experienced a real, frank, and simple conversation that was enough to relieve a certain inner conflict, to offer greater courage, to remove a burden, to share a great joy, to give advice that informs, reassures, and strengthens?

I wish that every young person had in their contacts list the number of a priest or a nun whom they trust, whom they can write to, and whom they can address without fear of being a bother or of being judged. Take the time to find the means to be "accompanied" rather than "driven" on this beautiful path that you are building for yourself. All alone, you can be deluded, and you can justify almost everything for yourself or become discouraged. Those who allow others to help them, who are willing to

confide in others, who accept that they sometimes need encouragement—they are the ones
who move forward. They are no less liberated.
Instead, they have at their fingertips the best
way to sustain their freedom, to strengthen and
preserve it.

Conclusion

It is time to end. Knowing that the enterprise of finding the time to read can be challenging for some, I promised myself not to write too much. Without having to repeat everything I have already said, I would like to encourage you to remember two things.

Once you have closed the book, take time to go visit a "padre"—or a sister—to take stock of your life. From all of what you have read, what do you remember? What would you like to change or improve in your way of life? You do not have to agree with everything that I shared with you. You must engage in the work of appropriation, to discern what will be yours to keep. This act of revisiting will give you the opportunity to mature your own beliefs, to facilitate a thought process that will deepen as you engage in more readings, in personal encounters, in friendly exchanges, and in your most personal prayers. This book will have achieved its goal not if it is read from cover to cover, but if it makes you want to pursue thinking for yourself— if it sows in your heart the desire to search for what is true, what is just, what is good in what you do, beyond your immediate desires. Such desires are not necessarily bad—without a doubt, they are often good—but they need to be subjected to discernment, that is, if you want to be liberated.

My second tip is to talk with your friends. Rather than posting a historical summary of your conquests and your heartthrobs (or pictures of these exploits) on your Facebook page, you can cultivate with your friends a desire for clarity. Encourage each other among friends. I have witnessed so many who confide in me their determination to show up for what is true but who cave in once they are seduced by the group effect, wishing to integrate with the group or under pressure from other people's approval. The group effect can also be positive when it leads us to do what is good. It is not about cultivating the "terror" of sin or the "fear of love." It is not either about imagining the same path for everyone, the same rhythm, and the same steps. It is instead about sharing a common imperative toward the same joy, to reassure and support each other, to encourage and motivate each other—not because one is better than the other, but precisely because we all know we have weaknesses and we are called to grow together on this path of true love.

I was always very touched to hear from young people that a particular friend's positive impact had provided the decisive effect. When two or three young people simply, joyfully, and honestly decide to be real in their relations, to preserve their bodies for the total gift of themselves, and to not fool around with easy tricks, then it is the whole group that is affected. If this proposal is not moralistically or sadly imposed on friends, but simply offered by young people who are happily alive, frank, open, and enthusiastic, then this happiness will not leave anyone indifferent. It will break any preconceptions and open new doors for those who do not know it. I truly believe that the best apostles for youth are the young people themselves.

"A Great Love Awaits Me"

How could we not end by turning toward Christ Jesus? In marriage or in a consecrated life, in a life of service to others or in a life of learning to love, we walk toward him as we continue our earthly pilgrimage. By loving, one way or another, we move toward this encounter, this face-to-face with the One who is the symbol of all Love: the One who loved us so that we can in turn love. This is the ultimate encouragement. Your life will not be successful because it will end in eighty years with a well-stocked bank account and diplomas hanging on the wall. Your life, whether it lasts fifteen, twenty, forty, sixty, or eighty years—who cares? It is not for us to decide. Your life will be beautiful and successful if you offer it as a gift. Your life will be successful if it leads to heaven after hearing this ultimate question of Jesus, perhaps the only one that He will ask at this point: "Have you loved? Did you really love me?"[1]

To love is to "give everything and to give oneself,"[2] as says St. Thérèse of Lisieux. I strongly believe that there is no other way of accomplishment and happiness possible for you, no other means to higher ground. This is what I wish for you: to be as you are, to prepare yourself for the joy of a complete gift by giving of yourself fully, wholeheartedly, and truthfully to what you are living. You are poor and weak, yet you have been called to live in love; you are made for the joys of the summit. Do not ever let anyone make you doubt it! Guided by Mary, Mother of Fair Love, star and clarity of our lives, dare to believe and to engage in it. Your joy will be there, your happiness will be there, there will be the joy of God!

Saint-Cyr-l'École,
Sunday, November 24, 2013
in the solemnity of Christ the King

Notes

Preface

1. Translator's note: The author did not provide a reference for this quotation.
2. Translator's note: The author did not provide a reference for this alleged quotation.

Introduction

1. Translator's note: A French Christian youth organization.
2. A copy of the text and audio recording of this talk can be found at http://www.padreblog.fr/. [Translator's note: Available in French only.]
3. Translator's note: The author did not provide a reference for this quotation.

Learning to Love

1. Translator's note: The author did not provide a reference.

Three Useful Sayings

1. Translator's note: The author used *small* instead of *friendly* in reference to the French expression *petit ami* or *petite amie*, literally "small friend," but it translates as "boyfriend" or "girlfriend."
2. Translator's note: The author did not provide a reference for this quotation.
3. Translator's note: The author did not provide a reference for this quotation.
4. Translator's note: "c" is likely short for *con*, which translates as "schmuck."

Quality Friendships

1. Translator's note: This translates as "Star on an Open Sea."
2. Translator's note: This was translated from the French secondary school system equivalent, *la première*, which is the middle of three years of high school.
3. Translator's note: A place of pilgrimage in eastern France.
4. On the issue of homosexuality, you can also read the letter from Philippe Arino on www.padreblog.fr: This young gay Christian explains why the Church's message seems just and true for him. [Translator's note: Available in French only.]

And What about God In All of This?

1. Translator's note: The author did not provide a reference for this quotation.
2. Translator's note: These words are the author's, not the actual Bible verse.

Conclusion

1. Translator's note: The author did not provide a reference for this quotation.
2. Translator's note: The author did not provide a reference for this quotation.

About the Author

Pierre-Hervé Grosjean is a French priest engaged with youth and questions of bio-ethics and politics. He is the founder and an author at padreblog.fr, a website offering straight forward Catholic answers to current issues and questions. Fr. Grosjean is a priest of the diocese of Versailles, and pastor of the parish of Saint-Cyr-l'Ecole. He is Secretary General of the Ethics and Politics Committee of his diocese. Often involved in the media, he is known for his use of social networks and the blog Padre-Blog. He founded the "Actors of Future" summer schools for students, to guide them in becoming tomorrow's Christian decision-makers. *Loving for Real* is his first book translated into English.

About the Publisher

The Crossroad Publishing Company publishes Crossroad and Herder & Herder books. We offer a 200-year global family tradition of books on spiritual living and religious thought. We promote reading as a time-tested discipline for focus and understanding. We help authors shape, clarify, write, and effectively promote their ideas. We select, edit, and distribute books. With our expertise and passion we provide wholesome spiritual nourishment for heart, mind, and soul through the written word.